m
Havana

Tower, Hotel Raquel, La Habana Vieja ©Sylvane Poitau/Apa Publications:

MICHELIN

mustsees **Havana**

Editorial Manager	Jonathan P. Gilbert
Editor	Gwen Cannon
Contributing Writers	Claire Boobbyer, Gwen Cannon, Françoise Klingen, Hans Maters, Anne-Marie Scott
Production Manager	Natasha G. George
Cartography	John Dear
Photo Editor	Yoshimi Kanazawa
Researcher	Glenn Michael Harper
Proofreader	Claiborne Linvill
Photo Research	Nicole D. Jordan
Layout	Nicole D. Jordan
Interior Design	Chris Bell, cbdesign
Cover Design	Chris Bell, cbdesign, Natasha G. George

Contact Us

Michelin Travel and Lifestyle
One Parkway South
Greenville, SC 29615
USA
www.michelintravel.com
michelin.guides@us.michelin.com

Michelin TravelPartner
Hannay House
39 Clarendon Road
Watford, Herts WD17 1JA
UK
(01923) 205 240
www.ViaMichelin.com
travelpubsales@uk.michelin.com

Special Sales

For information regarding bulk sales, customized editions and premium sales, please contact our Customer Service Departments:

USA	1-800-432-6277
UK	(01923) 205 240
Canada	1-800-361-8236

Michelin Apa Publications Ltd
A joint venture between Michelin and Langenscheidt

58 Borough High Street, London SE1 1XF, United Kingdom

© 2011 Michelin Apa Publications Ltd
ISBN 978-1-907099-45-8
Printed: August 2011
Printed and bound: Himmer, Germany

Note to the reader:
While every effort is made to ensure that all information printed in this guide is correct and
up-to-date, Michelin Apa Publications Ltd. accepts no liability for any direct, indirect or
consequential losses howsoever caused so far as such can be excluded by law. Admission
prices listed for sights in this guide are for a single adult, unless otherwise specified.

Welcome to Havana

La Habana Vieja

Introduction

A Timeless City   36

Must See

Districts   40
La Habana Vieja   40
Plaza de la Catedral   41
Plaza de Armas   45
Plaza de San Francisco   48
Plaza Vieja   50
Convento de Santa Clara   51
Convento de Nuestra
  Señora de la Merced   53
Iglesia de San Francisco
  de Paula   53
Convento de Nuestra
  Señora de Belén   53
Centro Habana   54
Malecón   54
Prado   55
Capitolio Nacional   55
Callejón de Hamel   59

Vedado   60
La Rampa   60
Universidad de La Habana 62
Castillo del Príncipe   63
Plaza de la Revolución   63
Cementerio de
  Cristóbal Colón   63
Miramar   65
Avenida Primera   65
Quinta Avenida   65
Marina Hemingway   67
Kohly District   67
Cuban Classics   68
Catedral de San Cristóbal 68
Instituto Superior del
  Arte School   69
Capitolio Nacional   69
Gran Teatro de La Habana 70
Hotel Sevilla   71
Coppelia   72
Edificio Bacardí   72
Hotel Nacional   72
Teatro América   73
Spanish Forts   74
Castillo de la Real Fuerza 74
Castillo de San Salvador
  de la Punta   75
Castillo de los Tres Reyes
  del Morro   76
Fortaleza de San Carlos
  de la Cabaña   76
Revolutionary Sites   78
Parque Céspedes   78
Parque de los Mártires   78
Museo de la Revolución   79
Plaza de la Revolución   80
Palacio de la Revolución 81
Museums   82
Art Museums   82
Museo Nacional de
  Bellas Artes   82
Museo de Artes
  Decorativas   84
Museo de la Cerámica   84
Museo de la Danza   85

Museums to Men	85
Museo José Martí	86
Museo Napoleónico	86
Museo Hemingway	87
Landmarks with a Beat	**88**
Café Cantante	88
Casa de la Música	88
Hotel Nacional	89
Casa de la Amistad	89
Callejón de Hamel	89
Sábado de la Rumba	90
Asociación Cultura Yoruba de Cuba	90
Delirio Habanero	90
La Zorro y el Cuervo	91
Cabaret Parisien	91
Tropicana	91
Café Taberna	91
El Jelengue de Areito	91
Parks and Gardens	**92**
Parque Central	92
Parque de la Fraternidad	93
Parque Lenin	94
Jardín Botánico Nacional de Cuba	95

p 12

Must Do

Outdoor Life	**108**
Performing Arts	**112**
Shopping	**116**
Nightlife	**124**

Must Eat

Restaurants	**128**

Must Stay

Hotels	**140**

Must Know

Star Attractions	**6**
Ideas and Tours	**12**
Calendar of Events	**18**
Practical Information	**22**
Index	**152**

p96

Best Beaches	**96**
Playas del Este	96
Best Excursions	**100**
Varadero	100
Matanzas	105
Las Terrazas	106

TABLE OF CONTENTS

★★★ ATTRACTIONS

Unmissable historic, cultural and natural sights

Instituto Superior del
Arte School   p 69

©Claire Boobbyer/Michelin

Cementerio de
Cristóbal Colón   p 63

©Claire Boobbyer/Michelin

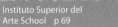

Plaza de Armas   p 45

©Claire Boobbyer/Michelin

Palacio de los Capitanes Generales   p 45

©Claire Boobbyer/Michelin

La Habana Vieja   p 40

©Abel Ernesto/Michelin

Catedral de San Cristóbal   p 68

©Claire Boobbyer/Michelin

ACTIVITIES

Unmissable activities and entertainment

Arts and crafts   p 121

Watch dominoes   p 111

Go sailing   p 111

Stroll the Prado   p 55

MUST KNOW

Relax at the beach (Varadero) p 100

©Claire Boobbyer/Michelin

Swing a golf club p 109

©Abel Ernesto/Michelin

Watch a baseball game p 111

©Abel Ernesto/Michelin

STAR ATTRACTIONS

★★★ ATTRACTIONS

Unmissable historic, cultural and natural sights

For more than 75 years people have used Michelin stars to take the guesswork out of travel. Our star-rating system helps you make the best decision on where to go, what to do, and what to see.

★★★	Unmissable
★★	Worth a trip
★	Worth a detour
No star	Recommended

★★★ Three Star

Catedral de San Cristóbal p 68
Cementerio de Cristóbal Colón p 63
Palacio de los Capitanes Generales p 45
La Habana Vieja p 40
Instituto Superior del Arte School p 69
Museo Farmacéutico p 106
Plaza de Armas p 45
Plaza de la Catedral p 41

★★ Two Star

Almacenes San José p 14
Calle Obispo p 47
Capitolio Nacional p 55
Casa de la Condesa de la Reunión p 44
Casa de los Marqueses de Aguas Claras p 42
Farmacia y Droguería Taquechel p 47
Gran Teatro de La Habana p 70
Hotel Sevilla p 71
Iglesia y Convento de Santa Clara p 51
Iglesia y Convento de San Francisco de Asís p 49
Malecón p 54
Museo de Arte Colonial p 45

Museo de Artes Decorativas p 84
Museo de la Ciudad p 45
Museo Nacional de Bellas Artes p 82
Palacio de Aldama p 94
Palacio de los Condes de Casa Bayona p 45
Palacio del Segundo Cabo p 46
Playa Santa María del Mar p 96, 98
Teatro Sauto p 106
Varadero p 100

★ One Star

Calle Oficios p 48
Callejón de Hamel p 59, 89
Casa de los Arabes p 48
Casa del Conde de Jaruco p 51
Casa del Conde de Lombillo p 44
Casa Natal de José Martí p 86
Casa del Obispo p 47
Castillo de la Real Fuerza p 74
Castillo de los Tres Reyes del Morro p 76
Cuevas de Bellamar p 106
Edificio Bacardí p 72
Fabrica de Tabacos Partagás p 58

Guanabo p 96, 98
Hotel Nacional p 61, 72, 89
Iglesia y Convento de Nuestra Señora de la Belén p 53
Iglesia y Convento de Nuestra Señora de la Merced p 53
Matanzas p 95, 105
Miramar p 65
Museo de la Cerámica p 84
Museo Hemingway p 87
Museo Napoleónico p 63, 86
Museo de la Revolución p 79
Palacio del Conde de Santovenia p 47
Palacio del Marqués de Arcos p 44
Palacio Presidencial p 79
Parque Central p 92
Playas del Este p 96
Plaza de San Francisco de Asís p 48
Plaza Vieja p 50
Prado p 55
Quinta Avenida p 65
La Rampa p 60
Las Terrazas p 107
Vedado p 60
Yumuri Valley p 99

MUST KNOW

ACTIVITIES

Unmissable activities, entertainment, restaurants and hotels

For every historic and natural sight in Havana there are many more activities. We recommend all the activities in this guide, but our top picks are highlighted with the Michelin Man logo.

Outings

Admire artifacts p 62
Drive along the
  Malecón p 54
Catch a coco-taxi p 30
Gawk at colonial
  buildings p 40
Relax at the beach
  p 96, 100
Stroll the Prado p 55

Hotels

Casa particular Candy
  Mederos y Alejandro
  p 146
Casa particular Eugenio
  y Fabio p 139
Casa particular Jesús
  y María p 140
Hotel Nacional p 145
Hotel Pullman p 148
Hotel Santa
  Isabel p 143
Meliá Varadero p 149
Palacio del Marqués de
  San Felipe p 143
Villa Los Pinos p 147

Nightlife

Ballet at Gran Teatro
  Habana p 110
Cabaret at Tropicana
  p 125
Cocktails in Bar
  Havana Club p 123
Dance the bolero p 91
Disco at Café
  Cantante p 124
Drama at Piso 9 p 113

Relax

Browse for books p 119
Have a drink with a
  view p 127
Eat ice cream p 62
Have hot
  chocolate p 50
See a puppet
  show p 115
Wander among
  palms p 95
Watch dominoes p 111

Restaurants

El Bodegón
  Criollo p 139
Doctor Café p 137
La Cecilia p 137
La Imprenta p 132
La Mulata del
  Sabor p 132
Mesón de la
  Flota p 132
El Patio p 133
El Templete p 133
El Tocororo p 138

Shopping

Art for purchase p 122
Arts and crafts p 121
Books aplenty p 123
Cuban coffee p 120
Cigar heaven p 120
Fancy fans p 123
Guayaberas galore
  p 122
Modern-day mall p 123
Musical offerings p 120
Pleasing produce p 120
Rum p 120

Splendid souvenirs
  p 121

Sports

Bike Old Havana p 31
Deep-sea fish p 109
Dive among coral
  reefs p 108
Float your boat p 108
Go caving p 106
Go sailing p 111
Play tennis p 110
Ride a zipline p 107
See a boxing match
  p 111
Snorkel p 111
Swim and sunbathe
  p 110
Swing a golf club p 109
Take a hike p 110
Watch a baseball
  game p 111

Side Trips

Hicacos Peninsula p 104
Matanzas p 105
Playas del Este p 96
Las Terrazas p 107
Varadero p 100

Underwater

Scuba dive p 108
Swim in a pool p 148
Tunnel to the Castillo
  de los Tres Reyes
  del Morro p 76
Watch fish at the
  aquarium p 66

STAR ATTRACTIONS

IDEAS AND TOURS

Throughout this thematic guide you will find inspiration for many different ways to enjoy your stay in Havana. The following is a selection of ideas to start you off. The sights in bold are found in the Index.

📹 WALKING TOURS

Havana is a great place to wander around, be it in the plazas of the Old Town, the ramshackle district of Centro, or the elegant mansion-lined avenues of Vedado. Distances between districts may warrant a taxi or botero. *The following self-guided walking tours are tailored to the sights found in Districts.*

La Habana Vieja★★★ (Old Town)

Allow 3 days. Havana's Spanish colonial old town is a UNESCO World Heritage Site. Sumptuous mansions, handsome churches, large convents and lively squares fill a warren of streets crammed high with residential apartments too. The Old Town's focus is the **Plaza de la Catedral★★★** ringed by the former houses of Spanish nobles as well as the Baroque cathedral. This district is full of

hotels in restored historic palaces, restaurants, bars, cafes, major as well as quirky museums, some boutique shops, and other cultural attractions. It can be properly accessed only on foot.

Centro Habana

Allow 1 day. Centro Habana is a vast, mostly residential district with buildings in states of disrepair; some structures are being restored. While Havana is one of the safest cities in the world, take precautions with bags and cameras when you are away from Centro's main roads, **Avenida Galiano** and the pedestrianized **San Rafael**. San Lázaro, a major throughway for traffic, is useful for finding taxis. The **Malecón★★** is Havana's long seawall and de facto open-air living room. Walk its length during the day and at dusk to see *habaneros* as they fish,

La Habana Vieja

©Paul Harris/John Warburton-Lee/Photononstop

MUST KNOW

play music and relax. Turn from the Malecón up the pedestrian tree-lined walkway **Prado★**, flanked by lion statues, lamps and marble seats. After passing the **Capitolio Nacional★★** and **Fábrica de Tabacos Partagás★**, turn right into **Barrio Chino** (Chinatown). To visit **Callejón de Hamel★**, the colorful alley of music, murals, and culture, take a taxi across town.

Vedado★

Allow 2 days. Vedado is a smart neighborhood with leafy avenues, mansions garlanded in bougainvillea, and music and cultural institutions. Its architectural elegance is exemplified in its museums and palaces of entertainment: the **Museo de Artes Decorativas★★**, **Museo Napoleónico★**, and **Casa de la Amistad**, all within reasonable walking distance of each other. Vedado begins at **La Rampa★** (Calle 23), a wide thoroughfare edged with clubs, airline offices, banks and the imposing Ministry of Sugar. At the sea end, the Art Deco **Hotel Nacional★** rises on a bluff; the nearby L-shaped **Edificio Focsa** offers one of Havana's best rooftop **views★★★**. The "palace" of ice cream, **Coppelia★**, and the palace of learning, **Universidad de La Habana,** are here. Some distances are too great to walk, so take a taxi.

Nuevo Vedado

Allow 1 day. South of Vedado is this residential zone. At its northern border are the monumental **Plaza de la Revolución**, and the Art Deco **Memorial de José Martí**. It is possible to walk from the plaza to the vast, shadeless **Cementerio**

de Cristóbal Colón★★★. Just north of here, at the western end of Calle 23, you will find refreshments and the cinema strip with Cuba's movie-making headquarters and Cafe Fresa y Chocolate.

Miramar★

Allow 3hrs. Take a taxi to begin a walk here. The main thoroughfare is **Quinta Avenida★** (Avenida 5). It is flanked by prominent mansions that were once the homes of Havana's wealthy, but now are mostly embassies, consulates, headquarters of foreign companies, and cultural institutions. Palm trees and benches line a central green median. Highlights include the **Maqueta de La Ciudad** There are few refreshment stops in this area.

OTHER WALKS
Revolutionary Tour

For a glimpse into Cuba's history, take this walking tour of the main revolutionary sights in the guide. Begin your tour at the statue of independence leader **Carlos Manuel de Céspedes** in Parque Céspedes within the **Plaza de Armas★★★**. Walk north on Tacón to the **Parque de los Mártires** to admire the statue of hero General **Máximo Gómez**. Facing this statue is the domed bulk of the old Presidential Palace, now the **Museo de la Revolución★**. Behind the museum stands an outdoor memorial to vehicles and weaponry, including the yacht **Granma**, which transported Fidel Castro and his band of rebels from Mexico to eastern Cuba in 1956. From Old Havana take a taxi to the **Plaza de la Revolución**. Climb the tower dedicated to independence

leader José Martí **(Memorial de José Martí)** and admire the iron sculptures of Castro's stalwarts, Che Guevara and Camilo Cienfuegos, on the buildings surrounding the plaza.

Made in Cuba

Start your morning walk with a drink! Begin the tour at the **Fundación del Ron** to learn about rum-making, and taste the national brand, Havana Club, in the bar next door. Walk west along Calle Muralla before turning right to Calle Cuba 513 to see the work of the silk-screen printing workshop **Taller de Serigrafía René Portocarrero,** where prints are for sale. Continue along Calle Cuba to Calle Armagura and turn right. At the corner of Calle Mercaderes stands the **Museo de la Cerámica★**, a new showcase for clay-making. Take a break in the **Museo de Chocolate**, which sits on the opposite corner. Cuban chocolate bon bons are made in front of customers, who sip hot chocolate or coffee (Cuba's cacao bean flourishes in the tropical east of the country). Head north up Calle Mercaderes and turn left on Calle

Obispo to visit **El Quitrín** on the corner of Calle San Ignacio; it sells the traditional man's white shirt with pockets *(guayabera)*. Continue north along San Ignacio to the Plaza de la Catedral to visit the **Galería del Grabado** inside the **Taller Experimental de Gráfica** at no. 62 Callejón del Chorro; here lithographs are made and work is also for sale. Return to Obispo before crossing Parque Central and making your way to **Fábrica de Tabacos Partagás★** at no. 520 Calle Industria. After a cigar and coffee at the in-house bar in the **Casa del Habano**, take a taxi out to **Estudio Taller José Fúster** in Jaimanitas *(Calle 226 and Avenida 3-A; 7 271 2932; www.josefuster. com)*. The ceramic artist's house and pool present a riot of colorful decoration. Clearly influenced by Gaudí and the *trencadís* ceramic mosaic artistry, his house is covered in fantastical creations.

Markets

Start your tour in Old Havana at the **Almacenes San José★★**, a one-stop arts and crafts market on Avenida del Puerto south of the Iglesia San Francisco de Paula,

Almacenes San José

©Claire Boobbyer/Michelin

between Calle Cuba and San Ignacio. Walk north on San Ignacio to the book and curios **market in Plaza de Armas**. Work your way up to *Calle Obispo 411, between Calle Compostela and Aguacate*, where **craft stalls** are set up in a vacant lot. From Obispo turn right *(north)* on Villegas to Empedrado to find the small indoor **agromercado, La Catedral** *(Empedrado, between Monserrate and Villegas)*; here fruit and vegetable sellers and the butcher are friendly (purchases are in *moneda nacional* CUP). There are agromercados at Calle 19 and Calle B in Vedado, as well as the largest at the **Mercado de Cuatro Caminos** *(Calle Matadero and Calle Monte, in Cerro; closed Monday)*.

Architectural Tour
Ascend to the rooftop bar at the **Hotel Saratoga** *(corner of Prado and Calle Muralla)* for a view of the Neoclassical **Capitolio Nacional★★**. Then walk past the building south along Prado to admire the Neo-Baroque façade of the **Gran Teatro de La Habana★★** embellished with statuary. Cross Parque Central to the corner of Monserrate and San Juan de Dios to view the Art Deco detail of the **Edificio Bacardí★**, but it is best viewed from the alfresco bar in the Hotel Plaza. Walk south on Prado to the Neo-Moorish **Hotel Sevilla★★** *(at Calle Trocadero)*. Check out its **interior** as well. Walk across Prado and continue on Trocadero until Avenida Italia (Calle Galiano). Turn left to the **Teatro América** *(253 Calle Galiano corner of Calle Concordia)*. Step inside to see the Art Deco interior. Take a cab to the Art Deco **Hotel Nacional★** before taking a break with an ice cream at the space-age modern **Coppelia★**. Be sure to arrange an appointment and a return taxi to visit the brick creations of the **Instituto Superior del Arte School★★★** *(1110 Calle 120, between Avenida 9 and Avenida 13, in Cubanacán)*.

OTHER TOURS
Guided Tours
For walking tours, the **Agencia de Viajes de San Cristóbal** offers a variety of historic, religious and architectural tours as well as socio-cultural tours. It can be found at most hotel desks throughout Havana (*www.viajessancristobal.cu*) Consider taking a **Hemingway Tour** as it covers all the bases with a guide and would cost you much more if arranged independently.

Antique Car Tours
Now that Cubans may rent their old American autos *(máquinas)*, some excellent tours of central Havana and its distant *barrios* are a fun way to explore the city. Ask at *casas particulares* for licensed drivers. The state-run **Gran Car** *(see p30)* also operates tours in polished old American autos.

Bus Tours
See HabanaBusTour p29.

LESSONS & CLASSES
Accommodations can be arranged through most of these organizations.

Dance
Danza Contemporánea de Cuba (www.dccuba.com) offers 2-week workshops (Taller Cubadanza) in modern Cuban dance, starting the first Monday in January and the first Monday in August. On a weekly basis, **Caledonia**

(www.caledonialanguages.com) offers group classes in salsa, reggaeton and tango, plus accommodations.

Conjunto Folklórico Nacional de Cuba *(www.folkcuba.cult.cu/laboratorio.htm)* holds beginning, intermediate and advanced 15-day classes in rumba, mambo, son, and cha-cha-chá as well as Santería (yorubá) dances.

Advanced classes learn dances of Congo origin, Palo y Makuta, and learn to sing Bantú. Every third Monday of January and every first Monday of July.

Ballet Nacional de Cuba *(www.festivalballethabana.cult. cu/paginas/catedra.html)* offers five ballet classes during the October-November biennial ballet festival for dancers with five or more years of ballet experience.

Paradiso *(www.paradiso.cu)* offers 2-, 3-week or 1-month courses in techniques in modern dance and ballet every July.

Paradiso *(www.paradiso.cu)* offers 1-, 2-, 3-week or 1-month courses in Cuban popular dance including contradanza, danzón, cha-cha-chá, mambo, son and rumba. Independent travelers may approach **Marisuri's School** in Centro Habana *(www.marisuri.com)* to arrange classes.

Instruments

Conjunto Folklórico Nacional de Cuba *(www.folkcuba.cult. cu/laboratorio.htm)* has 15-day classes for beginning to advanced students in percussion that include instruments for Yambú and Guaguancó rumba (Bombo, Tumbadoras, Sartenes y Claves). Every third Monday of January and every first Monday of July.

On a weekly basis, **Caledonia** *(www.caledonialanguages.com)* offers group percussion classes. **Paradiso** *(www.paradiso.cu)* offers 2-, 3-week or 1-month courses in **Cuban percussion** every July. **Paradiso** *(www.paradiso.cu)* offers 2-, 3-week or 1-month workshops on **guitar** in Cuban popular music every July.

Singing

Paradiso *(www.paradiso.cu)* offers 2-, 3-week or 1-month workshops on a repertory of **Cuban songs** every July.

Cuban Culture

The **University of Havana** offers monthly courses on the first Monday of each month *(www.uh.cu/infogral/estudiaruh/postgrado/english.html)*.

Spanish

The **University of Havana** offers monthly courses in all levels starting on the first Monday of each month *(www.uh.cu/sitios/cursos_academicos_internacionales/cursos_espannol)*.

Caledonia offers private and group classes *(www.caledonia languages.com)*.

Cooking

Restaurante La Casa *(865 Calle 30, between Calles 26 and 41, in Nuevo Vedado; 7 881 7000)* launched cooking classes in 2011 *(http://restaurantelacasacuba.com)*.

Painting

Paradiso *(www.paradiso.cu)* offers 1-, 2-, 3-week or 1-month classes in the art of Cuban **landscape painting**.

NATURAL SIGHTS

The **Río Alemendares** divides Vedado and Miramar. It runs through Parque Metropolitano de la Habana, which incorporates Parque Almendares and Bosque de la Habana. On weekends, guided tours are possible. There's also a children's play area, a skateboarding area and boat rides. In the city center, the **Parque Central★**, with its Royal palms and gardens, is close to the more urban **Parque de la Fraternidad**. On the city's southern outskirts stretches **Parque Lenin**, with limited attractions and an artificial lake. In the southern zones lies the **Jardín Botánico Nacional de Cuba**.

SIDE TRIPS

East of Havana stretch the white-sand beaches collectively known as **Playas del Este★**. Most visitors head for **Playa Santa María del Mar★★**; most Cubans head for **Guanabo★**. Beyond Playas del Este, also on the eastern beaches, is the cove of **Playa Jibacoa** and its solitary hotel. East of Jibacoa, the main road leads to **Matanzas★** and its **Teatro Sauto★★** and **Museo Farmacéutico★★★**. **Varadero★★** is Cuba's largest beach resort, with all-inclusive, internationally managed hotels. The main attraction is the picture-postcard paradise of white-sand beaches off a turquoise sea. For a glimpse of Cuba's birdlife and natural charm, head to **Las Terrazas★** in Artemisa province. The ecoresort of the same name sits in the mountains surrounded by forest, waterfalls and the ruins of coffee plantations. Guided walks and the **Hotel Moka** are the tourism mainstays.

Quick Trips

Stuck for ideas? Try these:

Aquatic Sports *108*
Art Galleries *122*
Ballet Performances *112*
Baseball Games *111*
Beaches *96, 100*
Biking *31*
Boating *102, 108*
Bolero *126*
Book Browsing *45, 123*
Bus Tours *29*
Cabaret *91*
Churches *52, 53*
Colonial Architecture *40*
Cuisine *130*
Culture *16*
Dancing *15, 89*
Ecotourism *107*
Festivals *18*
Fishing Trips *102, 109*
Folklórico *114*
Fortifications *63, 74*
Gardens *95*
Golf *109*
Hemingway Tour *15*
Hiking Trails *110*
Markets *14, 120*
Museums *82*
Nightlife *124*
Parks *92*
People-watching *45*
Performing Arts *112*
Puppet Shows *115*
Resort Hotels *100*
Revolutionary Sites *78*
Sailing *108*
Santería *39*
Scuba Diving *97*
Shopping *66, 116*
Snorkeling *97*
Tango Lessons *16*
Vintage Vehicles *48*
Waterside Stroll *54*
Zipline Ride *107*

IDEAS AND TOURS

CALENDAR OF EVENTS

Listed below is a selection of Havana's most popular annual events (dates and times may vary; check in advance). For details contact Infotur, the National Office of Tourist Information run by the **Cuban Ministry of Tourism:** *(7) 204 0624, (7) 204 6635 or www.infotur.cu*, **or** the **Ministry of Culture:** *www.min.cult.cu (in Spanish)*.

January/February

Liberation Day

Every *January 1*, celebrants come to Havana's **Plaza de la Revolución** to commemorate the historic day of liberation as a result of Fidel Castro's Revolution in 1959. The day is a public holiday for all Cubans.

Chinese New Year

Chinatown's grandest celebration is held the last week of *January* and *February 15*, when the lunar New Year is welcomed in by residents of Havana's **Barrio Chino**. Festivities include a dragon parade, fireworks, lion dances and family reunions. The **Cuban School of Wushu** also presents a display of martial arts.

Feria Internacional del Libro de La Habana

Sponsored in *February* by local bookstores and literary organizations, **Havana's Book Festival** means public readings, special presentations and browsing through lots of titles as well the announcement of the prestigious Latin American writers' awards. The main venue is usually **Fort San Carlos de la Cabana**. *www.cubaliteraria.com*

Festival del Habano

This popular event scheduled near the *end of February* sees the gathering of cigar lovers from all over the world for tastings, cigar-rolling lessons, factory tours, a gala dinner and other activities. *www.festivaldelhabano.com.*

March/April

Havana Bienal

Occurring every two years between *March and June*, this prestigious event brings contemporary art shows to the **Museo Nacional de Bellas Artes** and other locations in Old Town. The month-long cultural show is devoted to the art of Latin America and the Third World in all media. The next Bienal will be held May 17-June 12, 2012. *www.bienalhabana.cult.cu*

Varadero Gourmet International Festival

The Ministry of Tourism of Cuba and the Palmares S.A. invite the public to this food festival held at the **Plaza America Convention Hall** in Varadero *in early April*.

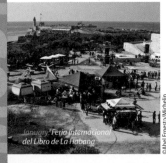

January: Feria Internacional del Libro de La Habana

©Abel Ernesto/Michelin

MUST KNOW

May/June
Primero de Mayo

A tribute to the workers of the world, the *1st of May* celebration is devoted to parades, political speeches and flag waving in Havana's **Plaza de la Revolución**, an event which draws huge crowds.

Festival Internacional de Poesía de La Habana

Sponsored by Cuba's Writers' and Artists' Union (Unión de Escritores y Artistas de Cuba), this *May event* attracts poets from around the world for readings and workshops as part of an international cultural exchange. *www.cubapoesia. cult.cu/wp.*

Cubadisco

One of the country's biggest musical events, **Feria Internacional del Disco** draws foreign production companies as well as Cuban music producers *every May* to this annual combination trade fair and festival. Concerts are staged primarily at **Pabellón Cuba** but occur throughout the city, and musical awards are handed out. *www.cubadisco.soycubano.com*

Ernest Hemingway International Blue Marlin Fishing Tournament

Sport-fishing aficionados descend on Marina Hemingway in *late May or early June* for this annual event hosted by the **Hemingway International Nautical Club** and started by the writer himself.

International Old Man and the Sea Billfish Tournament

Marina Hemingway is again a center for fishing fans at this annual tournament held in *early*

Carnaval de La Habana

©Sylvaine Poitau/Apa Publications

June. www.international hemingwaytournament.com

Coloquio Internacional Ernest Hemingway

Usually held every two years at the **Hotel Ambos Mundos** and **Museo Hemingway** around *mid-June,* this symposium focusing on the famed American writer is organized by the Consejo Nacional de Patrimonio Cultural. Many aspects of Hemingway's life and writings are presented and discussed, such as his fascination with bullfighting and his knowledge of Cuba. The next event will be held in 2013. *(7) 691 0809. mushem@cubarte.cult.cu.*

July/August
Carnaval de La Habana

The pinnacle of Havana's annual celebrations, **Carnaval** means evening parades with celebrants in creative costumes dancing to live music along the Malécon and in front of the Capitolio

19

Religious Festivals

Las Charangas de Bejucal (principally held December 24) are a mix of carnival, dance and sideshow held in the town of Bejucal, some 15km/9mi south of central Havana. Floats—up to 20m/65ft high and covered in lights—are created by two competing groups, La Ceiba de Plata and La Espina de Oro, which, over the course of the night, try to outdo each others' floats with more decoration and dancers garlanding the towering carnival structures. The origin of the rival groups dates back to the times when Roman Catholics and their black slaves took to the streets to honor their deities; today, membership into either group is based on family history or individual preference.

Nochebuena (December 24) is celebrated in churches throughout Havana and at home by Cubans who roast a pig in celebration. Each December 17 **St Lazarus' Day** is celebrated at the sanctuary of El Rincón, near Santiago de Las Vegas. Thousands of pilgrims come from Havana, many crawling all the way on their knees, to honor the patron saint of lepers and the poor. **Nuestra Señora de la Caridad** is the patron saint of Cuba. Her feast day (September 8) is celebrated with a procession in Centro Habana on the Sunday before this date, and at churches named in her honor. The feast of **Nuestra Señora de la Candelaria** (February 2) is celebrated at the Ermita de la Candelaria in Guanabacoa with a procession. The **Feast of San Juan Bautista** is celebrated between June 21 and 25 in San Miguel del Padrón; on June 24 an image of Saint John the Baptist is burned. The feast day is celebrated with music, food stalls and children's activities in this Havana municipality, located southeast of central Havana.

building on *August weekends*. Giant caricatures of popular figures called Muñecones and Gigantes are a highlight of the parades.

26 July (Revolution Day)

This important date in Cuba's revolutionary history, a public holiday, is honored with political speeches on TV, and patriotic banners and graffiti in the streets. It marks the **birthday of Cuban patriot José Martí**, as well as Fidel Castro's failed assault on the Moncada barracks in Santiago de Cuba in 1953.

September/October

Festival Internacional de Ballet

A highlight for ballet lovers around the world, this major biennial event, held in *late October through early November*, presents gala performances of both classical and modern ballet by various dance companies as well as the **Cuban National Ballet** at the **Gran Teatro de La Habana**, **Teatro Mella,** and **Teatro Sauto** in Matanzas. *www.festivalballethabana. cult.cu (in Spanish)*

Festival de Teatro de La Habana

Held in *October/November*, this 10-day **Theater Festival** is celebrated with performances of adult and children's plays as well as workshops in Havana's theaters. Cuban and international theater groups stage productions of Cuban classics as well as contemporary works. *www.fth.cult.cu.*

November/December

Nuestra Señora de las Mercedes

On *November 16*, Old Havana celebrates **Our Lady of the Mercedes**, while the founding of the city is commemorated with an ancient ritual in the **Templete garden.**

In front of El Templete is a ceiba tree that symbolizes the founding of the city. Citizens circle the tree three times, offer money, and embrace and kiss the tree.

International Latin American Film Festival

Held in *early to mid-December*, this 10-day **film festival** showcases the latest Cuban, Latin American and even Western productions. Screenings and seminars take place in dozens of cinemas in **Havana**, but mostly in **Vedado**, and are often followed by parties. The festival is headquartered at the Hotel Nacional in Vedado. *www.habanafilmfestival.com.*

Marabana Marathon

Held the *3rd Sunday of November each year*, this sporting event attracts thousands of runners from many countries to participate in a **half marathon** through Old Havana, Centro Habana and Vedado. The day before the marathon, the Maracuba, Cuba's largest running event, sees more than one million competitors in the race.

Salón Internacional de Arte Digital

Held in *November* in various city venues, this week-long event attracts practitioners of the **digital arts** to Havana for demonstrations, talks and exhibits of the latest technologies in the print and audio-visual media. *(7) 866 6585*. *www.artedigitalcuba.cu.*

Havana Jazz Festival

Held *four days in mid-December*, this renowned festival features local and International talent performing in such venues as the **Casa de la Cultura Plaza** and Teatro Nacional de Cuba. *www.festivaljazzplaza.icm.cu*

December: International Latin American Film Festival

©Abel Ernesto/Michelin

PRACTICAL INFORMATION

WHEN TO GO
Seasons

Lying just south of the Tropic of Cancer on the north coast of Cuba, Havana has a **subtropical** climate. Generally hot and humid year-round, the city experiences temperatures that average 22°C/72°F in winter and 27°C/81°F in summer.

Due to the island's narrow shape, temperature differences between Cuba's coast and inland areas are small. November to April is considered the winter **dry season** and May to October the summer wet season, during which thunderstorms are frequent but short. **Hurricane season** runs from June to November, with September and October posing the greatest risk. Your departure date depends largely on your interests. If you have visions of relaxing on white sand Caribbean beaches, east of Havana, **summer** is the best season to visit Cuba's capital. **Winter** is a better choice for travelers seeking insights into the island's colorful history, folklore and architecture. **February, March** and **April** may be a good compromise for visitors who want to escape the crowds of **peak season** (December-January and July-August), yet enjoy both outdoor and cultural activities. If you plan your visit to coincide with major festivals (see Calendar of Events), such as the Havana Carnival celebrated on August weekends, you'll need to buy your plane ticket and reserve accommodations far in advance.

What to Pack

It's advisable to take a swim suit and lightweight, casual clothes. Fast-drying, natural fabrics work best in Havana, where humidity is high all year, averaging 77 percent during the dry season, and 82 percent in the wet season. Some rainproof clothing and/or an umbrella are essential in the summer. A sweater or lightweight jacket will come handy on cool evenings (December and January) and protect you from freezing air-conditioning on night trains, buses and at some tourist sights. The island's prevailing dress code is laid back, but many Cubans like to dress up when going out at night. Men need not pack a tuxedo, since a long-sleeve shirt with nice trousers is considered acceptable.

Weather Forecasts

A weather forecast is part of the 8pm evening news on Cuban TV (in Spanish). The chief national newspaper, Granma, publishes daily weather forecasts (in Spanish). For weather and hurricane **forecasts: (7) 866 6060** (Spanish only).

Average Seasonal Temperatures in Cuba			
	Jan	**Apr**	**Jul**	**Oct**
Avg. High	27°C/81°F	30°C/86°F	32°C/90°F	32°C/90°F
Avg. Low	17°C/63°F	20°C/68°F	23°C/73°F	21°C/70°F

Infotur Office

KNOW BEFORE YOU GO
Useful Websites

www.infotur.cu – Cuba's official tourism website (English available) features practical information and maps, as well as Havana's lodgings, transportation, museums, entertainment and more.

www.bbc.co.uk/search/cuba – The British Broadcasting Corporation's site has the latest Cuban news, sports, cultural events.

www.cubanow.net– This site (in English) is devoted to articles about and offerings of Cuban art and culture, especially literature, cinema, visual arts and music.

www.cubaabsolutely.com – This site provides features and in-depth stories and a monthly downloadable calendar of events.

www.cubaweb.cu/en – The best feature of this site (in English) is its updated listing of cultural offerings on the island: music, theater, dance, comedy, exhibits, films, and such.

www.gocuba.ca/client/home/index.php – Informative, fairly comprehensive site of Cuba's Tourism Board in Canada (in English).

http://havanajournal.com – The Havana Journal (in English) features Cuban business, politics, culture, various directories, a photo gallery, and a travel forum.

http://lanic.utexas.edu/la/cb/cuba – This website is an online English version of the Latin American Network Information Center with links to all kinds of Cuba-related sites.

Tourism Offices

Instead of the usual tourist offices, Cuba has a network of **state-run tour** agencies such as Havanatur, Cubanacán, Cubatur and Sol y Son, along with the offices of **Infotur**, the official **tourist information bureau** run by the Cuban Ministry of Tourism. These agencies make hotel reservations, help with bus transportation (Víazul, Transtur) and car rentals, but principally sell tours and excursions.

If you need sightseeing advice, upscale hotels usually have a small **information desk** that will direct clients to the city's finest restaurants/*paladares*, best stores or major sights.

www.infotur.cu – The official website of the National Tourist Information Office of the Ministry of Tourism of Cuba.

Infotur Offices in Havana
There are several locations in the capital city:
524 Calle Obispo, between Calles Bernaza and Villegas (La Habana Vieja), *(7) 866 3333* (Map II, A3) *9am–1pm, 1:45pm–5pm.*
Conveniently located in downtown Havana, the office on Calle Obispo offers the best service, but it is not tourism information as we know it.
Calle 112, corner of Avenida 5 (Miramar), *(7) 204 7036* (Map V, off the map), *9am–5pm.*
Small information kiosk with variable hours at corner of Calles Obispo and San Ignacio (La Habana Vieja) (Map II, B2).
At **José Martí International Airport**: *(7) 266 4094.*
Major tourism agencies **Cubatur**, *www.cubatur.cu* and **Havanatur**, *www.havanatur.cu*, have information desks in Havana's major hotels.

Tourist Assistance
Asistur (Map II, A2), Prado # 208, between Colón and Trocadero (La Habana Vieja), *(7) 866 4499, www.asistur .cu. Emergency numbers 24 hrs daily, (7) 866 8339, 866 8527 to 8529, or 866 8920.*
Contact this insurance company if you lose your ID, require hospitalization, or have failed to arrange approved medical insurance prior to arrival. Financial and legal assistance is available.

International Visitors
Cuban Embassies Abroad
Cuban Consulate Office and Cuban Interests Section –
2630 16th St NW, Washington DC 20009, *202 797 8518, www.cuba diplomatico.cu/sicw/EN/Home.aspx*

Embassy of Cuba in Canada –
Consular Section 5353 Dundas West, Square Kipling, Suite 205, Toronto, Ontario; *416 234 8181; www.cubadiplomatica.cu/canada*
Cuban Embassy (UK) – 167 High Holborn, London, WC1V 6PA; *020 7240 2488; http://emba. cubaminrex.cu/Default.aspx?alias= embacuba.minrex.cu/inglaterraing*

Foreign Embassies in Cuba
British Embassy – 702 Calle 34, between Avenidas 7 and17, Miramar (Playa), Havana; *(53) (7) 214 2200 or (53) (7) 204 1771; http://ukincuba.fco.gov.uk*
Canadian Embassy – 518 Calle 30 at Avenida 7, Miramar (Playa), Havana; *(53) (7) 204 2516 (general), (53) (7) 204 7097 (request temporary residence visas only); www.canada international.gc.ca/cuba*
US Interests Section – Calzada between Calles L & M, Vedado, Havana; *(53) (7) 833 3551 through 59, emergencies (53) (7) 833 2302; http://havana.usint.gov*

Entry Requirements
Entry requirements to Cuba are subject to change and **vary significantly**, depending upon the traveler's nationality.
US citizens are not in the same category as Canadian or British nationals. For example, **US citizens are prohibited from spending money** (in any currency) **relating to Cuban travel** unless they are licensed by the US Department of the Treasury Office of Foreign Assets Control (OFAC), or are Cuban Americans with close relatives in Cuba. For information, access *www.treasury.gov/resource-center/ sanctions/Programs/Pages/ cuba.aspx.*

Prior to departure, visitors should check with the Cuban mission in their own country as to the conditions that apply to their personal case. You may want to visit the official site of the **Ministry of Foreign Affairs of Cuba**: *www.cubaminrex.cu/ English/RecommendedWebsites/ RecommendedSites.html*. From the listing of the Cuban missions abroad, select the one located in your native country, and navigate through the section devoted to consular affairs, which includes reliable, current information *(in Spanish and English)* about passports and visas. Since there are restrictions on US citizens' travel to Cuba, US travelers should visit the official US government website: *www.travel.state.gov* for details. A **valid passport** is required from any foreign visitor entering Cuba. Also see Health below for insurance requirements for entry into Cuba. In lieu of a visa, a **tourist card** *(tarjeta del turista)* is also needed for all visitors, including minors traveling under their parents' passports. The tourist card, which will be collected by Cuban authorities upon your leaving the country, can be obtained at Cuban missions abroad prior to departure. Most travel agencies include the tourist card in their package and will purchase it for you; be sure to ask in advance. In the UK, you can also purchase it from *https://secure.visacuba. com/pages/home.aspx*. To get this important document, you must submit a valid passport (or a legible photocopy of the first four pages), proof of return/onward travel (or a certificate issued by your airline or travel agency showing your arrival/ departure dates) and payment

of the processing fee. With a few exceptions, the tourist card is valid for a single-entry vacation trip of up to 30 days, but may be extended for an additional 30 days once in Cuba.

To obtain a **visa extension**, you will need to purchase bank stamps *(sellos)* at the Banco de Crédito y Comercio (also known as Bandec), the Banco Metropolitano or the Banco Financiero Internacional, and bring them along with your passport and the tourist card that needs to be extended, to the **Dirección de Inmigracíon y Extranjería** in Havana *(203 Calle 17, between Calles J and K, Vedado, 53 7 206 3218, or Calle186 between Avenida 5 and 1, Reparto Flores.* It is wise to call ahead or preferably to get someone to call on your behalf, since extension fees vary. Temporary visitors to Cuba can also travel on **business** or **student visas** *(check www.cubaminrex.cu/ English/RecommendedWebsites/ RecommendedSites.html for specific requirements).*
Never overstay your visa, if only by one day, as you may end up in custody, since Cuban immigration authorities take any breach of their rules and regulations seriously.

Vaccinations

No vaccination is officially required to travel to Cuba, unless you arrive from a country where yellow fever is present, in which case you will be asked to show an international vaccination certificate stating that you are currently immune.
In addition, the CDC online Health Information for Travelers at *wwwnc. cdc.gov/travel/destinations/cuba* recommends that visitors to Cuba be up to date with routine shots

such as tetanus, measles and polio, and that they be protected against hepatitis A, hepatitis B, typhoid and rabies.

Should visitors stay in Cuba for an extended period (three months or more), they will have to take an **HIV test**.

Customs Regulations

Before you depart for Cuba, visit the official site of Cuban Customs (English version available) at *www.aduana.co.cu/ingles/turista3.htm* for a full listing of **prohibited,** dutiable and controlled items upon entry and exit. Provided their total weight is below the limit authorized by your airline, personal belongings such as cameras, laptops and regular prescription drugs (a copy of the prescription will facilitate entry through customs) may be carried into Cuba without having to pay import duty. If you plan on bringing gifts and don't want to pay taxes on them, their total value must not exceed 50CUC.

Importing drugs, firearms and explosives into Cuba is strictly prohibited, while processed or non-processed products of animal or vegetable origin are subject to requirements. Reading material deemed to be a threat to the nation may be confiscated upon your arrival in Cuba, so choose your paperback novel wisely.

You may bring back home only two bottles of rum, and 20 cigars without proof of purchase or up to 50 cigars in their original container sealed with the official hologram; over that amount, you'll need to submit the invoice.

Note: If you are a US citizen, your rum and cigars will be confiscated upon entering the US. According to www.travel.state.gov, only books, films, photos, artwork, posters, tapes and CDs, with the exception of blank tapes and CDs, are allowed back into the US.

Exporting a living specimen of an endangered species or a product made from one without a permit carries a hefty fine and confiscation, as does National Heritage works (such as rare books).

Health

Health insurance, with provision for emergency repatriation, is compulsory for visitors to Cuba to cover potential medical expenses for the period of their stay.

To enter the country, all visitors to Cuba must carry **proof of health insurance**, such as insurance policies or certificates, medical assistance cards valid for the period of stay and issued by a Cuban government-approved organization to show that whatever medical assistance they may need in Cuba will be duly paid back. Failure to produce such proof carries a charge of 2.5CUC per person a day.

Travelers without adequate health coverage will need to purchase Cuban health insurance upon arrival *(http://europa.cubaminrex.cu/English/LookCuba/Articles/Others/2010/06-04.html)*.

Since US insurance company policies will not provide coverage in Cuba, US citizens should access www.travel.state.gov to see what recourse they have. Upon leaving the country, visitors with unpaid medical bills may be detained by Cuban authorities.

The great number of **public hospitals** in Havana serve mostly

Cuban patients. Diplomats and foreigners tend to go to the **Clínica Central Cira García**, 4101 Calle 20 and Avenida 41 *(Playa,* Map V, B1, *between Miramar and Kohly; 7 204 28 11 to 14; www.cirag.cu/ingles/ index.htm)* with its English-speaking staff. The care is expensive but high-quality, and payment must be made in CUC. The clinic's pharmacy is better stocked than most other pharmacies in the city.

Should you run out of medicine, some of the major hotels in Havana such as the Plaza *(7 861 5703) (see Hotels)* have their own pharmacy and doctor on call. Don't forget to take prescription and over-the-counter drugs you think you may need for your trip, and bring your own personal hygiene products as well.

GETTING THERE
By Air

José Martí International Airport is located 18km/11mi south of downtown Havana by way of Ave. Rancho Boyeros.
International flight information: *(7) 266 4133 or 642 0100.*
Domestic flight information: *(7) 266 4010.*

Terminal 2 *(7 266 4431)* is used by the increasing number of US charter flights now flying to Cuba. **Standard taxi rate** between the airport and downtown is 25CUC. Since the majority of **US citizens** are not permitted to visit Cuba, there are no scheduled flights on major airlines from the US. If you have obtained a license from the US Treasury Department, or are a Cuban American meeting the rules, charter flights to Havana are now available from 12 US airports, including Miami, Los Angeles and New York, which can be booked through Travel Service Providers (TSPs) *(see Tour Operators below).* A good general source of information is *www.cubatravelnetwork.com/ en/flights/cuba flights.asp.*

Airlines

From Canada, **Air Canada** has daily flights to Havana from Toronto; for fares and schedules www.aircanada.com. **Cubana de Aviación** has regularly scheduled flights to Havana from Toronto, Halifax and Montreal; for fares and schedules, access *www.cubana.cu/ home/?lang=en.*
From the United Kingdom, **Virgin Atlantic Airways Ltd.** has regularly

José Martí International Airport

©Abel Ernesto/Michelin

scheduled flights to Havana from London's Gatwick airport; *www.virgin-atlantic.com.*
Cubana de Aviación runs regularly scheduled flights from London to Havana; fares and schedules: *www.cubana.cu/home/?lang=en.*
Cubana de Aviación requires all passenger baggage to be shrink-wrapped in plastic on flights from Havana; wrapping service is free of charge. Other airlines offer (but do not require) shrink-wrapping for a small fee (8CUC). **Cubana de Aviación** (Map IV, B1), *64 Calle 23 and Calle Infanta (Vedado), (7) 834 44 46. Open Mon–Fri 8:30am–4pm; Sat 8:30am–noon. Airport office (7) 649 0410.*

Ground Transportation
Taxis and hotel shuttles for guests (shuttle reservations are a must) are available. Taxi rates from the airport are standardized based on what part of Havana you are going to, so do not plan on negotiating the fare beforehand.
Expect to pay as much as 25CUC for the one-way trip from the airport to Vedado, and up to 30CUC to La Habana Vieja. The return trip from Havana to the airport will cost you less: about 15CUC from Vedado, and a bit more from La Habana Vieja.

Airline Information
Most major airlines operate offices located in the vicinity of the **Rampa** *(Calle 23, Vedado)*. (Map IV, B1) or in the **Centro de Negocios, Miramar.**

Tour Operators
Several tour operators and licensed Travel Service Providers offer full trip-planning and reservation services for Havana. Here is a sampling by country:

US: ♦ **Center for Cuban Studies** – This nonprofit New York City-based organization specializes in trips for humanitarian missions and educational purposes. *www.cubaupdate.org.*
♦ **Marazul Charters Inc.** – This Travel Service Provider, licensed by the US government, has been arranging trips to Cuba for licensed travelers for more than 30 years. *www.marazulcharters.com*

UK: ♦ **Journey Latin America** – Seasoned staff plans affordable, tailor-made tours for individuals and groups, including flights and hotels. *www.journeylatin america.co.uk*
♦ **Cuba Direct** – Customized travel service, including flights, hotels, car rentals and escorted tours run by a UK-based Cuban outfit. *www.cubadirect.co.uk*
♦ **Captivating Cuba** – has a long history of offering tailor-made tours to Cuba. *www.travelzest.com/en/tour-operators/view/brand/Captivating%20Cuba/cuba*
♦ **Esencia Experiences** – offers insider tours of Cuba to the discerning traveller: *www.esencia experiences.com*
♦ **STA Travel** – International experts in discounted travel for young travelers/students (under 26 years of age), including flights, transportation and lodging.

GETTING AROUND
By Air
Cubana de Aviación runs daily flights between Havana and Santiago de Cuba, Holguín,

Camagüey and Nueva Gerona; and several weekly flights to other Cuban cities.

By Train

Havana's main rail station, **Estación Central de Ferrocarriles** *(Map II, B4; 7 862 4971)*, lies south of Old Havana, on Egido. Daily departures for all main cities on the island. Trains are slow, unreliable and often full; due to potential and numerous breakdowns, they should not be used by tourists on a tight schedule.

Tourists are served at a special office along the rails, across from the corner of Calles Aresenal and Cienfuegos; tickets are available for purchase in CUCs.

All trains make space available for tourists. **Regular** trains run during the day; **especial** trains run at night. From Havana to Santiago (13hrs) is about 50CUC. Reserve seats at least a day in advance.

By Bus

The Víazul bus, designed for tourists, is comfortable, reliable and air-conditioned; reservations can be made online. **Víazul** (Map IV), *corner of Calles 26 and Zoológico (Nuevo Vedado), (7) 881 1413, www.viazul.com*. The bus station is located about 10km/6mi from **Old Havana** *(5–6CUC for a taxi to the station)*. Purchase tickets at any agency or at the tourist office at least a day in advance in high season. Be at the station 1hr before departure.

Points of service from Havana include: **Varadero** *(via Matanzas and the Varadero airport, 3hrs, 10.80 CUC);* **Trinidad** *(via Cienfuegos, 5hrs35min, 27CUC).*

Viajes Cubanacán offers door to door transfers from Havana to Varadero, Viñales, Cienfuegos, Trinidad and Santiago at prices equal to Víazul; make reservations at hotel tourist desks.

Transtur *(www.transtur.cu)* operates the **HabanaBusTour** in Havana daily 9am–9pm. It consists of hop-on/hop-off red buses (double-decker open-top buses) following two different tourist routes. All-day tickets are valid on each line. **Line 1** serves the historic center of Havana to the Plaza de la Revolución (5CUC). **Line 3** serves Old Havana, Parque Central, and the beaches east of Havana, ending at Santa María del Mar (3CUC).

At **Terminal de Ómnibus Interprovinciales**, Havana's interprovincial bus terminal, located on Avenida Ranch Boyeros, north of the Plaza de la Revolución, chaos is the norm, with teeming crowds of people at all hours of the day. Víazul buses pull in here. The local buses (known as **guaguas**) run infrequently, and long lines form at bus stops; avoid them at all costs if you're in a hurry. One-way tickets cost 40 Cuban pesos (CUP).

HabanaBusTour

©Claire Boobbyer/Michelin

Coco taxi

©Patrick Frilet/age fotostock

By Taxi

Several types of taxi services operate in Havana. The official state-run company **Cubataxi** *(7 855 5555)* offers long-distance service to destinations in and outside the city. Private old American cars for hire are less expensive, but are often in poor condition. When negotiating with the driver, ask if the cost of gasoline is included in the price. Cubataxi stops are located at most tourist attractions. Rates are payable in CUCs and are officially regulated by meter; trips start at 1CUC. If the meter is broken, negotiate the price with the driver before departing (experience and knowledge of standard rates helps in this regard). A less expensive option, unmetered **private taxis** *(taxis particulars)* are operated by drivers in their personal vehicles—often 1950s American makes or Russian-made Ladas with a "Taxi" sign in the windshield. Known as *boteros*, these colorful cabs drive up and down major avenues and carry as many passengers as possible. Most of these taxis ply Havana's main arteries on set routes, stopping when hailed. It is now legal for *boteros* to accept fares from foreigners; whether you have the language skills to ask for the route you want is another matter. From Avenida de Los Presidentes to the Capitolio costs around 10CUP; from anywhere east of the Almendares River under the tunnel to Miramar and beyond is 20CUP.

For short trips around the center of town, options include two-passenger bici-taxis and coco-taxis. **Bici-taxi** carriages are powered by bicycle, and drivers solicit fares from foreigners now that it is legal to do so; fares are payable in CUC. **Coco-taxis** are three-wheeled vehicles painted bright yellow and powered by a driver on a moped; fares are not metered and are

Important Phone Numbers
Do not assume the following numbers will be answered by an English-speaking person

Emergency (ambulance)	☏ **(7) 838 1185** or **838 2185**
Police	☏ 106
Fire	☏ 105
Asistur emergency number *English speaking staff available*	☏ (7) 866 4499

exorbitant. You pay for the novelty factor; fares are payable in CUC. **Gran Car** *(7 881 0992)* is the official, state-run agency for old American car rentals.

The vehicles are in beautiful condition. Rates run from 25CUC an hour including driver and are best booked through the hotel desks facing Parque Central or by hailing the ones that park outside Hotel Parque Central.

By Car

Although there are several national car-rental companies operating in Havana, it's best to reserve well in advance, especially if you're visiting during the tourist season.

The three main companies are: **Cubacar** (Map IV), *corner of Avenida 3 and Paseo (Vedado),* (7)833 2164; **Havanautos**, *corner of Calles 23 and H (Vedado)* (Map IV, A2), *(7) 837 5901*; **REX**, *corner of Avenida 5 and Calle 92 (Miramar)* (Map V, A1), (7) 209 2207, or *corner of Calzada and Malecón (Vedado)* (Map IV, A1), *(7) 835 6830*, or *Terminal de Cruceros (Old Havana)* (Map II, C3), *(7) 862 6343*. Car-rental offices can also be found at the airport and major hotels.

By Bicycle

Bikes are useful for exploring the narrow streets of Old Havana, and Vedado, where attractions are spread out.

Bicycle Rentals: WoWCuba MacQueen's Island Tours, Centro de Negocios Kohly *(Salon 2, Calle 34, between Calles 49 and 49A, Reparto Kohly; 7 698 0041 Mon–Fri, 5 272 1777 cell pm/urgent, www.wowcuba.com)*.

All rentals must be reserved and prepaid in advance through the company's Canadian office. There is a 3-day minimum rental requirement for independent rentals. Rates for the services/ equipment are detailed there. Detailed quotes, reservation information and payment options can be obtained by completing the online Bicycle Rental Quotation form. Theft/breakdown insurance is not offered by WoW in Cuba. To protect equipment and minimize risk, customers are advised to bring a lock and use official bicycle parking *(parqueo)* payable in CUP.

Cyclists looking for longer-term rentals are advised to bring with them: a basic multitool, minipump with Presta/Schraeder fittings (if your pump is Schraeder only, a Presta adaptor is recommended). A universal water bottle and spare tubes are also a good idea to have.

ACCESSIBILITY

Because of limited funding and resources, Cuba lags behind when it comes to amenities for the mobility challenged. There isn't much in the way of specially equipped **transportation**.

As for hotels, some do have ramps and wide doors, and others such as the newer all-inclusive resorts offer high standards of accessibility to their disabled guests, but these establishments are the exception rather than the rule.

For information about wheelchair access and special needs transportation, contact **Infotur**. Its main office is located at *524 Calle Obispo, between Calles Bernaza and Villegas, in Old Havana* (Map II, A3). *(7) 866 3333. www.infotur.cu.*

BASIC INFORMATION
Accommodations
For suggested lodgings, see Hotels.
Infotur lists a number of Havana hotels on its website: *www.infotur.cu.*
Online real-time availability can be viewed on *http://www.cuba hotelreservation.com.*

Hotel Reservations
Infotur, Cubatur
(www.cubatur.cu) and most tour operators offer reservations services. Many of the city's major hotels can be reserved online through their own websites.

Business Hours
Banks
Weekdays 8am–3pm (long lines are common).
Cadeca exchange offices *(see Money below)* are open *Mon–Sat 8am–6pm, Sun 8am–1pm.*
Outside of office hours, you can exchange money in the lobbies of most major hotels.
Stores – *Mon–Sat 10am–6pm*. Boutiques in hotels are generally open daily until 7pm.

Museums/Tourist Attractions
Opening times and weekly closing days greatly vary, depending on the type of sight, but many are open *Tue–Sun 9am–5pm, Sun 9am–1pm*. Some churches are open only during mass.

Post Offices
Mon–Sat 8am–5pm. Mail service is provided by major hotels 24/7.

Restaurants and Paladares
Daily 11:30am to about 11:30pm. In small provincial towns, restaurants may close early.

Electricity
Less frequent than in the past, power outages *(apagones)* still occur throughout the island. Tourists rarely are inconvenienced because hotels have their own generator. In the *casas particulares*, candles, flashlights or fluorescent battery-powered lanterns are the rule. The most common voltage in Cuba is 110 volts (60 Hz), with power outlets generally suited for use with North American flatpin plugs (with or without a grounding pin, depending on the case). In newer hotels and some casas particulares, you may find 220-volt power requiring a European type of ungrounded plug with two round pins.

Internet
Connections are very slow and breakdowns are frequent. Decent yet expensive service is usually provided by business centers in major hotels, where prices may be as high as 15CUC per hour (in Miramar), less in Old Town. ETECSA, the national telecommunications company, also provides Internet access (with frequent connection problems though) in Telepunto kiosks such as the one on the corner of *Calles Obispo 351 and Habana* (Map II, B2), *open 8:30am–5:30pm, 6CUC per hr.* However, the best action is to buy an ETECSA card at one of the central hotels for 6CUC for one hour's use. The card is valid for 30 days. A card bought in a hotel can only be reused in the same hotel. A card bought at an ETECSA office can be reused at any ETECSA office. There is also access at the new craft market. Be warned that Cubans have very limited, government-controlled, **national**

Internet access (basically limited to a simple email service), and that allowing them to use your **international Internet access** may get them into trouble. Note that you must now show your passport to buy an Internet card. It is not always requested, but is now fairly common practice.

Wi-Fi is available in very few places in Havana. It's cheapest in Centro (at Hotel Parque Central) at 8CUC per hour and more expensive in hotels in Vedado and Miramar.

Mail

Most major hotels offer postal, telephone, Internet and photocopying services, for a fee; you may have to pay a lot for the convenience. **Correos** (post offices) can be found in **Old Havana** *to the left of the Gran Teatro (*Map II, A3) *and at Plaza San Francisco de Asís* (Map II, C3).

DHL offices can be found on **Calzada,** *between Calles 2 and 4 in Vedado, and at the corner of Avenida 1 and Calle 26 in Miramar.* (Map V, B1).

Money
Cuban Currency

Two currencies are in circulation in Cuba: the **Cuban national peso** (CUP) and the **Cuban convertible peso** (CUC), which, to add to the confusion, coexist under the same dollar symbol of $. The convertible peso is distinguished by the words "Peso Convertible"; the national coins and notes bear the words "República de Cuba." The Cuban peso, the national currency *(moneda nacional),* will not be of much use to you, except for small purchases at a market or from street vendors; rides on carriages,

buses, or ferries; telephone booth charges; or the daily *Granma* (a national newspaper). Travelers to Cuba are required to pay for tourism services (hotels, restaurants, airline tickets, car rental, etc.) in convertible pesos. Cubans themselves need to use CUC to buy products not found in state stores. You will quickly learn to distinguish the shops, hotels and restaurants using *moneda nacional* that cannot normally accept foreigners because of licensing requirements: they are spartan and run down.

The convertible peso (CUC) consists of banknote denominations of 1, 3, 5, 10, 20, 50 and 100CUC and coins of 1, 5, 10, 25, 50 and 100 centavos (100 centavos = 1 peso). Small bills are always preferable--up to 10CUC. Be careful with your money, especially in markets, where prices may appear to be shown in convertible peso currency because of the dollar sign, but transactions are made in Cuban pesos.

At the time of publication, 1 CUC was equivalent to 1.00 US dollar, .69 Euro (1 Euro=1.44CUC), .61 GBP (1GBP=1.63CUC), .95 CAD (1 CAD=1.04CUC), .94 AUD (1AUD=1.05CUC).

Banks/Currency Exchange

All major hotels have currency exchange desks. You can withdraw money using your credit/debit card (at exorbitant fees) or exchange cash or travelers' checks at most banks (note : travelers' checks and credit cards drawn on US banks are not honored in Cuba). However, it is highly advisable that you **check with your credit-card issuer before your departure** to assure that your card will be accepted in

Cuba. **Banco Nacional de Cuba** (Map IV, B1, *La Rampa and Malecón, Vedado)*, **Banco Financiero Internacional**, Map IV, B1, *Calles Línea and O, Vedado);* Hotel TRYP Habana Libre *(Map II, C3; Calle Oficios at Brasil, Old Havana);* Centro Comercial Carlos III *(*Map IV, B2, *Avenida Salvador Allende, between Retiro and Arbol Seco).* State-run **Cadeca** counters exchange convertible pesos for Cuban pesos, and exchange foreign currency for convertible pesos: *257 Calle Obispo* (Map II, B2), *Calles Lamparilla and Oficios (Old Havana)* (Map II, C3); *Avenida 5 and Calle 42 (Miramar)* (Map V, A1).

You can withdraw convertible pesos from several ATM machines in Havana, including at some Cadeca offices. Note : All exchanges between CUC and US dollars are subject to a 10 percent Cuban tax in addition to other exchange fees. It is best to bring as much cash in sterling, Euros or Canadian dollars to Cuba that you feel comfortable carrying.

Public Toilets

Public facilities should be avoided if possible. Most hotels and restaurants permit tourists to use the toilets in their common areas; be sure to leave a tip if there is an attendant. Be forewarned: most facilities don't have toilet paper, so always carry your own. To prevent clogged plumbing, dispose of paper in the bin provided.

Smoking

Serious smokers may want to try dark-brown tobacco cigarettes from Cuba. Some US brands can be found at tourist stores, hotel bars and gas stations (expect to pay 1.50CUC for a pack of mild cigarettes). Smoking is officially banned in public places such as hospitals, offices and theaters. Designated smoking areas exist in some hotels and restaurants.

Taxes

There are no official taxes in Cuba apart from the 25CUC departure tax. Some restaurants and paladars add a 10 percent service charge to customer bills.

Tips

Tipping *(propina)* has become a common practice in the tourism sector. It constitutes a significant additional salary for employees paid in pesos, such as parking attendants, museum guides, hotel maids, restaurant and hotel staff. Drivers of state-run taxis should also be tipped. Tip between 50 centavos and 1CUC, or even more depending on the service rendered, but avoid exorbitant tips. In some restaurants and paladars, a 10 percent service charge is not uncommon; check before you tip to see if such a charge has been added to your bill.

Telephone

The best way to avoid excessive hotel charges on local and international calls is to use one of the public **ETECSA** blue phones. They work with calling cards that can be purchased from any ETECSA office or Telepunto kiosks. Cuba's national telecommunications company, ETECSA, operates the blue telephone booths and Telepunto kiosks (some equipped with Internet capability); you will find them along Havana's streets. ETECSA sells prepaid calling cards (with scratch-off access codes) in amounts of 5, 10, 15, 20 or 25CUC for international calling (expect to pay 1.40CUC or higher per minute for international calls).

International Calls: To call Havana from outside the island, dial the appropriate international access code (Canada and US 011, UK 00, Australia 0011) followed by 53 (for Cuba) plus 7 for Havana and then the 6- or 7-digit local number. Cuban mobile numbers begin with 5. Dial 0 for operator assistance. For directory inquiries, dial 113. Calling collect is now possible; dial 180 for assistance. International prefixes include 1 (US, Canada), 44 (UK), and 61 (Australia).

Calling from your hotel room: 88 + your country's international prefix + number (no 0 prefix).

Calling from a card phone: Dial the 166 access code followed by your card's scratch-off code, then by the # pound sign (or hash key), then by 119 + your country's international prefix + number (no 0 prefix), then by the # pound sign.

Calling from a Cuban mobile: 119 + your country's international prefix + number (no 0 prefix).

Local Calls: To make a local phone call, you can use public phone booths that work with **pre-paid cards** in Cuban currency (CUP). The cheapest alternative is to use one of the older public telephone booths with a slot that takes CUP coins (Cuban pesos). For other domestic calls, use any card phone (make sure you keep CUC cards for international calls only however) and call from an ETECSA telephone center or from a phone booth at your hotel. With a card, dial the 166 access code followed by your card's scratch-off code, then by the # pound sign followed by the number you wish to dial.

Major hotels usually have a **fax** machine. Expect to pay about 15CUC for sending a fax. Most of the time, you'll have to pay for receiving one as well (1CUC/page).

Calling within the same city (local call): Dial the number (no area code needed).

Calling another city or province (intercity call): 01 + city/province area code + number.

Cell/Mobile phones – Cubacel (www.cubacel.cu) is the country's mobile telephone company. You might be able to use your own phone, given Cubacel's extensive roaming coverage; check with your service provider before departing for Cuba. Otherwise, you can rent a phone or rent a SIM card at a Cubacel office (at the airport in Terminal 3 or in Vedado at Calle 17 and C) or at a Telepunto kiosk (see Internet above).To call a cell phone from a landline, dial the prefix 05. To call another cell phone from a cell phone, dial the prefix 5.

Time

Cuba is in the Eastern Standard Time zone (same as Miami). Daylight Saving Time is observed from mid-March to late October.

Water

Water is supposed to be potable in tourist areas, but it is highly recommended that you drink only bottled water, which is for sale in most tourist restaurants and bars, as well as in shops. Avoid consuming street food and beverages containing water. Be wary of ice, even in the finest hotels—and ask if the water served has been boiled.

PRACTICAL INFORMATION

A TIMELESS CITY

Sitting just south of the Tropic of Cancer in the Atlantic Ocean, Havana occupies a northwest location on the largest of the Caribbean islands, Cuba. The city stretches westward and southward from a natural bay, accessed by a narrow inlet that protects the harbors therein. West of the bay, the Almendares River bisects the city from south to north. Cuba itself projects westward into the Gulf of Mexico, halfway between Florida to the north and Mexico. This strategic location led the Spanish conquerors to call Cuba "the key to the Gulf." The country's—and Havana's—fate has long been tied to its geographic position.

The political, cultural and financial capital of Cuba as well as a major port, Havana is a slowly modernizing metropolis of some 2.2 million ethnically diverse people. Though it seems preserved in a vacuum, the city is decidedly modern when compared to other Cuban cities. Luxury hotels here have many of the amenities expected of top international destinations. Wireless spots in hotels, though still few in number, may soon increase when Cuba joins the rest of the connected world with the July 2011 switching on of the subaqua fiber optic broadband cable between Cuba and Venezuela. **Tourism** is on the rise and a number of cultural exchanges, commercial trade fairs and sporting events continue to attract international visitors, to the financial benefit of the city.

Havana Fast Facts

Area: 721sq km/278sq mi
Year of Founding: 1519
City Population: 2.2 million
Annual Visitors: (to Cuba) Approx. 2.5 million
Airlines Servicing City: 19
Havana's Port: Handles half of Cuba's trade

You won't find many ultramodern buildings in Havana, or a profusion of lighted signs, ads or a shopping center on every corner. But Havana's antiquated charm holds great appeal for visitors. Despite years of economic sanctions and the resulting shortages, the people of Havana, the *habaneros*, have a ready smile. Music can be heard in nearly every nook of the city, and live salsa bands always draw crowds. By night the capital emerges from the day's tropical languor, and revs up to a nightlife charged with **Afro-Cuban rhythms**.

Havana holds its visitors spellbound for many reasons, but it is the city's mixture of **architectural styles**—from Spanish Colonial and Moorish to Neoclassical and Art Deco—that makes the place seem so timeless. Splendid façades evoke a glamorous but faded past, especially along the waterfront—the crumbling but magnificent **Malecón**—where sun, seaspray and tropical downpours have dimmed, but not erased, a palette of pastel colors. Behind the seafront lies the city's colonial core, a labyrinth of alleyways, cracked sidewalks and dilapidated but still grand buildings, overhung

Havana's Diverse Population

Ever since Cuba was first colonized, successive waves of immigration have resulted in a mingling of different races with the **indigenous peoples** who were on the island at the time of Columbus' landfall. Most of the Europeans who colonized Cuba were **Spaniards.** There were sharp distinctions between people from Spain and those of Spanish origin born in Cuba, referred to as *crillos* (creoles). At the end of the 18C, **French** immigrants arrived, fleeing the slave revolt on Haiti. A century later, incoming fortune-seekers from Europe included people from France, Germany, Italy and Great Britain. Cuba's past link with what was formerly the Soviet Union meant an influx of **Russians,** a number of whom have remained here. From the 16C to the abolition of slavery in 1886, **West Africans** were shipped to Cuba as slave labor. Intermarriage between slaves and Hispanics saw the rise of the *metizo* population. A person of mixed race in Cuba is known as a mulatto—a large portion of the population. The **Chinese** presence in Cuba is visible in Havana's *barrio chino* (Chinatown); ships bringing Cantonese workers first landed in Cuba in 1847. Today the Chinese comprise only about .1 percent of the population, however.

by headily scented flowers. To the west, a few skyscrapers and once-fine villas mark wide avenues where luxuriant tropical vegetation seems to smother everything with its exuberant growth.

In the streets, **American-made automobiles** from the 1950s compete for pride of place with run-down Russian Ladas, yellow coco-taxis, bicitaxies, and an expanding fleet of modern vehicles. Everywhere you'll see *habaneros* lining up to squeeze aboard overloaded buses known as *guaguas*.

Every year on November 16, in the gardens of El Templete, the people of Havana commemorate the anniversary of the **founding** of their city. On this day, in 1519, Spanish conquistadors held a solemn Mass to mark the founding of the town of **San Cristóbal de la Habana,** which had been moved twice from its original site. The town is said to have been named for **Habaguanex**, a native chief, although some historians believe the name derives from the word "haven" in reference to the harbor to whose development the city's fortunes have been closely tied.

©Claire Boobbyer/Michelin

Gran Teatro and 1950s American autos

The town's strategic position between the Americas and Spain proved a boon to economic growth. Tradesmen set up shop around the harbor to gain access to ships loaded with sugar, gold, silver, tobacco, slaves, and precious minerals. In the wake of these wealth-laden ships, however, came pirates and buccaneers in the pay of Spain's European rivals. Between 1538 and 1544 the **Castillo de la Real Fuerza** was constructed to protect the city from incessant pillaging. Despite such measures, Havana was seized in 1555 by Jacques de Sores, a French privateer. New fortifications were quickly built, and commerce flourished more than ever. In the mid-16C, Cuba's rulers moved the seat of government from Santiago de Cuba to more prosperous Havana, which became the official **capital of Cuba** in 1607.

Havana was attacked repeatedly by the British throughout the 17C and 18C. On August 13, 1762, the city fell into the hands of the English after two continuous months of siege. Less than a year later, under the terms of the Treaty of Fontainebleau, Cuba was transferred back to Spain in exchange for Florida.

At the end of the 18C, the whole of the American continent was gripped by the desire for independence. By 1825 only Puerto Rico and Cuba remained under Spanish rule. Slavery continued to be a mainstay of colonial society; final emancipation came in 1886, following the end of the first (1868-1878) of two **wars of independence**. The explosion aboard the **USS Maine** in Havana harbor in February 1898 prompted the US to send troops to Cuba. Spain was soon defeated, and formally gave up its colony at the signing of the **Treaty of Paris** on December 10, 1898, at which no Cuban delegation was present. More than a half a century

View of the Capitolio in 1929

© Bettmann/Corbis

The Island's Main Religions

Cuba is a secular country in which freedom of worship is guaranteed, though after the Revolution, an attempt was made to marginalize religion in national life. In 1991, however, the 4th Communist Party Congress decided that Party members should again be free to practice the religion of their choice. In 1996 Fidel Castro was received at the Vatican by Pope John-Paul II, and in 1998 the Pope's visit to Cuba was a major event that also saw Cuba reinstate Christmas Day as a public holiday.

Spanish colonial rule ensured that **Roman Catholicism** became the country's dominant religion. In addition to its many Catholics, Cuba has around 500,000 **Protestants,** the result of North American influence in the early part of the 20C. There is also a small **Jewish** community that maintains three synagogues in Havana. One small mosque, Havana's only one, serves Cuba's **Muslim** population.

Santería, the religion practiced by the Yoruba people of southeastern Nigeria, has a substantial number of followers in Cuba. An example of increased official tolerance of Santería in recent times was Fidel Castro's formal welcoming of the ruler of the Yoruba to Cuba in 1987. Covering a range of Afro-Cuban beliefs, Santería emerged in the country when imported African slaves fused the worship of African deities with Roman Catholicism. About 20 of the 400 Yoruba *orishas* (gods) are worshipped in Cuba. Special ceremonies are occasionally held for the benefit of tourists as well as the State, which gains hard currency as a result.

---

later, the **Cuban Revolution** (1953-59), led by Fidel Castro and Che Guevara, is seen by some as belated revenge for this snub to a proud country.

In the 19C Havana grew beyond the historic boundaries of its fortifications, which except for the defenses at the harbor entrance, were largely demolished in 1863. Development bypassed the city's historic heart, which became known as **La Habana Vieja** (Old Havana), and centered instead on newer districts to the west, such as **Centro Habana.** After Cuba became a republic in 1902, **Vedado** and **Miramar** saw major development. Letters and numbers were used to designate streets in these districts, which were laid out on a grid similar to American urban plans. American investors erected luxury hotels, gambling casinos and magnificent villas along the Almendares River. Following the **Revolution** *(see Revolutionary Sites)*, the city was purged of its casinos and brothels, and many of the elegant mansions were requisitioned away from private ownership.

Recent years have seen a rise in tourism in Cuba. Modern hotels are being upgraded to cater to international visitors, and additional grand colonial buildings in Old Havana, a **UNESCO World Heritage Site**, are being painstakingly restored.

More and more *habaneros* are opening their homes as lodgings and as family-run restaurants to serve the growing tourism trade.

DISTRICTS

Havana stretches out along the Straits of Florida on the northwest edge of Cuba. The coastal city is divided into 15 administrative districts called *municipios*, but for sightseeing purposes, the following four geographical areas capture the major attractions of interest to visitors: La Habana Vieja (Old Havana), Centro Habana, Vedado and the suburb of Miramar, each with its individual character, architectural styles and rhythm. Wear your most comfortable walking shoes and see Old Havana on foot. Less compact, the other three areas require four-wheel transportation to access. Composites of Havana's history, all mirror periods in the city's nearly 500 years of existence.

LA HABANA VIEJA★★★

Facing Havana Bay, La Habana Vieja, or Old Havana, stretches east from Paseo de Martí (known locally as the Prado) to the harbor, and to the southwest beyond the central train station to La Regla district. Partly enclosed by a ring road that follows the footprint of ancient fortifications, Old Havana's historic heart holds the vast majority of

the city's ⚓ **colonial bulidings**. A stroll through its narrow streets reveals a rich architectural heritage that earned this part of the capital UNESCO World Heritage status in 1982. Much restoration work is ongoing today.

Pleasing Plazas

Four historic plazas, or public squares, continue to be the focal

LA HABANA VIEJA
Historic Center
Map III

0   50   100 m
0   50   100 yds

HOTELS		RESTAURANTS			
Ambos Mundos	①	Al Medina	①	Moneda (La)	⑥
Florida	②	Barca (La)	④	Patio (El)	⑤
Santa Isabel	③	Bodeguita del Medio (La)	②	Templete (El)	⑦
Tejadillo	④	Cafe O'Reilly	③	Torre la Vega	⑧

MUST SEE

Catedral de San Cristóbal

©Toño Labra/age fotostock

point of life today, and are worth a **walking tour** *(best to allow 2 days to complete it)*: Plaza de la Catedral, Plaza de Armas, Plaza de San Francisco de Asís and Plaza Vieja. Keep an eye out for the newly renovated colonial buildings along the way.

Plaza de la Catedral★★★

Initially called Plaza de la Ciénaga (Swamp Square), this square would become waterlogged in the rainy season back in the 16C. In 1587 a cistern was built on the square to supply the local population and passing ships with fresh water. Five years later, the neighborhood was connected to the **Zanja Real** (Royal Aqueduct) via the "royal channel" that ran through a dead-end street known as Callejón del Chorro (Water Stream Alley) on the southwest side of the square. A true masterpiece of colonial design, the plaza was renamed in the 18C after its most prominent building. By then, the square had been drained, and this prime location, close to the harbor and the Palace of the Captain Generals

(see below), attracted wealthy families who built fancy mansions around the plaza. Some of the mansions have been converted to museums.

◆ **Catedral de San Cristóbal★★★**
Open Mon–Fri 11am–2:30pm, Sat 10:30am–1pm, Sun 9:30am–12:30pm. Mass Sun 10:30am. Access to the bell tower 2CUC.
The cathedral is best seen on a sunny day, when the edifice is bathed in golden light, enhancing its form and architectural details. Framed by asymmetrical towers,

Touring Tip

The best way to take in the **view** of the Plaza de la Catedral and fully appreciate its layout is to get there early in the morning, before the usual hordes of tourists and musicians show up. Not only will you beat the crowd, but, if you come right after a storm, you will catch the reflections on the glittering cobblestones in the early morning light.

DISTRICTS

41

the Cuban Baroque **façade★★** is carved of fossil-embedded stone. The original church was erected by Jesuits in 1727. After the king of Spain expelled the Jesuit Order from Cuba, the enlargement of the church was completed by Franciscans in 1777; in 1788 the church was upgraded to cathedral status.

Its name honors **Christopher Columbus,** whose remains were reputedly brought from Santo Domingo and kept in the cathedral until removed to Spain upon Cuba's independence.

The **interior,** restored in the Neoclassical style, has a central nave and two aisles opening onto chapels. Above the **high altar★**, made of Carrara marble, are **fresco paintings** by Italian painter Giuseppe Perovani. The mahogany **retable** features martyrs and apostles. Those who won't have the opportunity to visit the city of Santiago de Cuba can see a copy of the famous **Virgen de la Caridad**

El Patio courtyard, Casa de los Marqueses de Aguas Claras

©Sylvaine Poitau/Apa Publications

del Cobre (Cuba's patron saint) in the cathedral.

◆ Casa de los Marqueses de Aguas Claras★★
Located on the west side of the square, this elegant mansion (1775) now holds the popular **El Patio restaurant** *(see Restaurants).*

HOTELS

Beltrán de Santa Cruz....... ①
Casa Colonial Azul............. ②
Casa Nancy Pérez............... ③
Conde de Villanueva......... ④
Convento de Santa Brigida y Madre Isabel...... ⑤
Dos Hermanas - Yonaika y Yonaisis............. ⑥
Eugenio y Fabio................. ⑦
Casa Humberto.................. ⑧
Inglaterra........................... ⑨

Jesús y María........................ ⑩
Olga López Hernández......... ⑪
Palacio O'Farrill.................... ⑫
Palacio San Felipe................ ⑳
Parque Central..................... ⑬
Plaza.................................... ⑭
Maritza Mirabal y Ramón...... ⑮
Residencia Santa Clara.......... ⑯
Saratoga.............................. ⑰
Sevilla.................................. ⑱
Valencia................................ ⑲

RESTAURANTS

Café del Oriente................. ①
Floridita (El)....................... ②
Casa de la Parra (La)........... ③
Imprenta (La)..................... ④

Mesón de la Flota................. ⑤
Mulata del Sabor (La)........... ⑥
Taberna de la Muralla (La).... ⑦
Torre del Oro........................ ⑧

Its lovely inner **courtyard**★ has a fountain, and its balcony offers a sweeping **view**★ of the plaza. On the same side of the square, **Casa de Baños** (formerly the Public Baths) was built in the 19C on the site of the cistern built in 1587. The ground floor has

been turned into an art gallery. At the corner of the building, the **fountain** of Callejón del Chorro brought water to the neighborhood long ago. Situated at the end of the Callejón del Chorro, the **Taller Experimental de Gráfica** is a

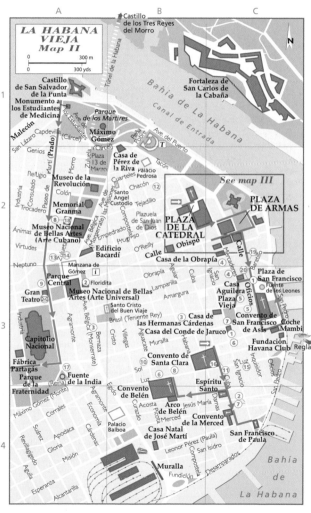

LA HABANA VIEJA Map II

0 — 300 m
0 — 300 yds

A B C

N

Castillo de los Tres Reyes del Morro

Bahía de La Habana

Canal de Entrada

Fortaleza de San Carlos de la Cabaña

Castillo de San Salvador de la Punta

Monumento a los Estudiantes de Medicina

Malecón

Parque de los Mártires

Máximo Gómez

Casa de Pérez de la Riva

Palacio Pedrosa

Plaza 13 de Marzo

Museo de la Revolución

Santo Angel Custodio

Memorial Granma

Museo Nacional de Bellas Artes (Arte Cubano)

Edificio Bacardí

See map III

PLAZA DE ARMAS

PLAZA DE LA CATEDRAL

Obispo

Casa de la Obrapía

Plaza de San Francisco

Fuente de los Leones

Manzana de Gómez

Floridita

Parque Central

Gran Teatro

Museo Nacional de Bellas Artes (Arte Universal)

Casa Aguilera

Plaza Vieja

Santo Cristo del Buen Viaje

Casa de las Hermanas Cárdenas

Casa del Conde de Jaruco

Convento de San Francisco de Asís

Coche Mambí

Capitolio Nacional

Fundación Havana Club

Regla

Fábrica Partagás

Convento de Santa Clara

Parque de la Fraternidad

Fuente de la India

Espíritu Santo

Convento de Belén

Arco de Belén

Convento de la Merced

Palacio Balboa

Casa Natal de José Martí

San Francisco de Paula

Muralla

Fundición

Bahía de La Habana

DISTRICTS

43

Over decades, Havana's historic buildings showed signs of advancing decay. Today several structures are now getting much-needed facelifts, and their former grandeur is slowly being restored. As you walk through the Plaza de Armas, Plaza Vieja, Calle Mercaderes and Calle Oficios, you'll see the conservation efforts that are being made. But many other buildings are in dire need of restoration. An enormous task lies ahead for the **Oficina del Historiador,** the supervisory body in charge of Old Havana's rehabilitation. Its financial resources come partly from taxes on hotels and restaurants operating within the district. Funds generated from them are directly reinvested into the *municipio* for the improvement of living conditions as well as cultural development through the Habaguanex organization (*www.habaguanex.cu*).

leading graphic arts workshop selling Cuban contemporary works of art and offering instruction in the art of engraving. One of the most popular bar-restaurants in Havana, **La Bodeguita del Medio** *(215 Calle Empedrado; see Restaurants)* sits just 50m/164ft west of the cathedral, on Calle Empedrado (between Cuba and San Ignacio).

◆ **Casa de la Condesa de la Reunión★★**

With its pleasant **patio★** and unusual **staircase**, this colonial mansion (c.1820), close to La Bodeguita del Medio, houses the **Fundación Cultural Alejo Carpentier** *(open Mon–Fri 8:30am –5pm)*, dedicated to the celebrated Cuban author (1904-80). Part of Carpentier's novel *El siglo de las luces* (1962) is set in this mansion. Regarded as one of Latin America's greatest historical novels, his work deals with the impact of the French Revolution on the Caribbean.

◗ *Walk to the northeast side of the plaza.*

◆ **Casa del Conde de Lombillo★**
Open Mon–Sat 9am–5pm.

This early 18C mansion, with a porch overlooking the plaza, was built for a family who made a fortune in the slave trade. The Baroque interior has been tastefully restored to its former splendor. Home of the City Historian's Office *(see sidebar Work in Progress)*, the building now stages exhibits in the galleries surrounding the inner courtyard. Built on the southeastern corner of the square in 1741, the **Palacio del Marqués de Arcos★** boasts an elegant Baroque façade graced with wrought-iron balconies and stately columns. The Royal Treasury was transferred here in 1796, as was the postal administration, in the first half of the 19C—note the **antique mailbox** built into the outside wall, similar to the one found on Calle Obispo *(see below)*. This heritage building was once home to Havana's College of Arts and Literature.

◆ **Palacio de los Condes de Casa Bayona★★**

Directly opposite the cathedral, the oldest mansion on the square was built in 1720 for **Luis Chacón**, military governor of Cuba. The Havana College of Notaries, a newspaper called *La Discusión* and a rum distillery were among the occupants of this palace from the second half of the 19C on. It now houses the collections of domestic and religious furniture and decorative arts of the **Museo de Arte Colonial**★★ *(open daily 9am–6:45pm; 2CUC)*, which offer insight into Cuba's colonial era (17C–19C). Architectural elements such as wrought-iron gates, wooden balcony railings and door knockers are part of the museum's treasures. You'll also see a few *mediopuntos*, colored glass or woodwork placed over windows in half-moon style to filter out light. The building itself has exquisite **stained-glass windows**.

▷ *Exit the square south along Calle San Ignacio, and walk east along O'Reilly to Plaza de Armas.*

Plaza de Armas★★★
Havana's oldest plaza (1582) was originally used for military parades and maneuvers, hence its name. It remained at the center of political life until the island gained formal independence in 1902, and continued to play a significant role in Cuban politics well into the first half of the 20C. The plaza was enlarged to its present size in the second half of the 18C, landscaped and graced with fountains, benches and street lamps. Over time, it fell into decline, but was entirely renovated in the mid-1930s. The centerpiece is a monument to **Carlos Manuel de Céspedes** (the "Founding Father" who initiated the wars of

independence), carved by Sergio López Mesa in 1955.

Today, Plaza de Armas attracts hosts of people drawn by its bohemian atmosphere and languid vibe. Royal palms and **ceiba** (or kapok) trees *(see sidebar on p 47)* shade the **central garden**, and sounds of music from the Cuban traditional repertoire waft over the square. Browse at one of the makeshift stalls that sell second-hand books, curiosities and Cuban memorabilia before settling in at a terrace cafe for some people-watching.

♦ **Palacio de los Capitanes Generales**★★★ **(Museo de la Ciudad**★★**)**
Filling the plaza's entire western side, this palace is a masterpiece of 18C Cuban Baroque architecture, designed by **Antonio Fernández de Trebejos y Zaldívar** *(see Palacio del Segundo Cabo)* and Pedro Medina. The square, thick-walled

Palacio de los Capitanes Generales

©Claire Boobbyer/Michelin

Museo de la Ciudad

building was erected on the site of Havana's first parish church (c. 1550), and took its present form in 1834, when major alterations were made. Home to the colony's Spanish governors until 1898, the strategic building was used for a while by American governors during the post-independence occupation of Cuba by the US. In 1902 it officially became the presidential palace of the Cuban Republic, filling this function until 1920. The building was also the seat of Havana's municipal government for 176 years. In1968 the old palace was turned into the **Museo de la Ciudad**★★ *(open Tue–Sun 9:30am–4:30pm; 3CUC)*, a repository for paintings, documents, weapons, furniture and memorabilia that illustrate the main periods in Cuban history. Rooms open onto a lush **inner courtyard**★★ with a statue of Christopher Columbus in its center. On the ground floor, the island's oldest colonial vestige, a **cenotaph** marks the death of a governor's daughter in 1557. A model of a sugar mill *(ingenio)*

depicts the 19C process of making raw sugar from cane. On the upper floor, the former rooms of the governor's residence are appointed with exquisite furniture, delicate china and fine paintings. The very first Cuban flag is on view on this floor, as is Cuban painter Armando Menocal's (1863-1941) work *Antonio Maceo's Death*, depicting the last moments of the independence hero in 1896. The official end of Spanish rule was proclaimed in the Salon de los Espejos in 1899.

⬥ **Palacio del Segundo Cabo**★★
Closed for renovation.
In 1772 the Royal Post Office *(Casa de Correos)* was built in the northwest corner of Plaza de Armas, alongside the Castillo de la Real Fuerza *(see Spanish Forts)*. Designed by Antonio Fernández de Trebejos y Zaldívar, this handsome building included not only the postal administration, but also the General Accounting and Treasury Office of the army. It was named Palacio del Segundo Cabo when it became the residence of deputy

governors in 1854. In the 20C, the building held the Senate and later, the Popular Supreme Court (1929), not to mention a number of academies and other institutions.

◆ El Templete
This tiny Doric-columned temple *(open Tue–Sun 9:30am–5pm; 1.50CUC)* was the first Neoclassical-style construction in Havana. It was erected in 1827 on the site where the **first mass** was celebrated, back in 1519. In 1753 a hurricane uprooted the **ceiba tree** *(see sidebar)* under which this memorable event took place and where the founding of Havana was commemorated each year on November 16. The following year, Governor F. Cajigal de la Vega had a column raised to mark the spot. The November 16 celebration is still held in the garden today *(see Calendar of Events)*, under another stately ceiba tree.
Inside the temple, notice the tryptich by **Jean-Baptiste Vermay** (1786-1833) depicting the first mass, the first city council and El Templete's inauguration.

◆ Palacio del Conde de Santovenia★ (Hotel Santa Isabel)
Across the street, the late-18C palatial mansion with wrought-iron balconies was converted to an inn in 1867; today it houses the luxury hotel, the **Santa Isabel** *(see Hotels)*.
Bordering the south side of Plaza de Armas, **Calle Obispo★★** is Havana's oldest street. A bishop *(obispo)* from a neighboring diocese gave his title to this narrow shopping street that begins at the plaza and ends near Parque

---

The Ceiba Tree
Also known as the kapok, or cotton, tree, the **ceiba** [pronounced SAY-bah] is a large tropical tree that is in the same family as the African baobab tree. Among the tallest in a tropical forest, the ceiba can grow as high as 60m/197ft. It is distinguished by its umbrella-shaped canopy and thick, cylindrical trunk (up to 3.5m/ 12ft or more in circumference). The tree's sizable above-ground roots resemble buttresses. Pollinated in part by bats, ceibas flower and bear fruit when their leaves fall off.

Central. The famous *calle* is lined with an eclectic mix of restored buildings, art galleries, museums, cafes, bars, hotels, restaurants and shops, some of the latter often poorly stocked.

▶ *Walk down Calle Obispo about two blocks to get the flavor of this busy street.*

On the corner of Calle Mercaderes, you'll see **Ambos Mundos** *(see Hotels)*, the hotel Hemingway stayed in for 8 years; the rooftop terrace makes a pleasant place to have a drink.
Nearby at number 155 Calle Obispo, the old French pharmacy known as **Farmacia y Droguería Taquechel★★** *(open daily 9am–7pm)* is graced with chandeliers and shelves lined with majolica jars. Its fascinating collection of pharmaceutical and medical antiques includes a water purifier, a dispensary table and the inevitable skeleton in a display case.

DISTRICTS

Farmacia y Droguería Taquechel

©Claire Boobbyer/Michelin

▷ *Return along Calle Obispo to Plaza de Armas.*

The **Museo Nacional de Historia Natural** *(open Tue–Sun 9:30am–7pm; 3CUC)* hosts school children who come to learn about the earth, mammals, birds, reptiles, fossils and more. If you are a nature lover, be sure to see the upper floor, which is devoted largely to species that are endemic to Cuba.

▷ *Walk south along Calle Oficios.*

◆ **Calle Oficios★**

Lined with renovated buildings housing a number of museums, this street heads south from Calle Obispo. On the corner **Casa del Obispo** (no. 6) includes La Mina restaurant and an ice cream parlor. At no. 8 the former **Palacio Abiscopal★** is a 17C colonial building boasting a beautiful inner courtyard. Its exquisite stained-glass windows are visible from inside the Centro de Información. It was home to Havana's bishops

until the first half of the 19C, when it was converted to a *monte de piedad* (pawn shop). It now houses the Office of the Historian of Cultural Patrimony for Old Havana. At No. 12 Calle Oficios, **Al Medina** restaurant *(see Restaurants)* occupies the former Colegio de Humanidades de San Ambrosio of 1689, a school of religious instruction for boys; the restaurant is set around a lovely inner courtyard covered with vine. Adjoining it, at No. 16, **Casa de los Arabes★** *(open Tue–Sat 9am–5pm, Sun 9am–1pm)* displays fine pieces of Islamic art that President Fidel Castro received as gifts from the heads of various Middle Eastern countries. Designed in Mudejar style, this "House of the Arabs" is Havana's only mosque; it retains a minaret and the original **prayer hall**, which is used on Fridays. Across the street, at 13 Calle Oficios, a converted late-19C warehouse is now home to the **Depósito del automóvil** *(open daily 9am–7pm; 1CUC)*. This interesting car museum is filled with vintage American automobiles such as Pontiacs and Thunderbirds, and includes classics like a 1912 Model-T Ford, as well as cars belonging to noted figures such as music legend Benny Moré.

▷ *Walk south on Calle Oficios to reach the next plaza.*

Plaza de San Francisco de Asís★

Located close to the waterfront, this vast cobbled square is a pleasant place for a cool drink or a meal at a sidewalk cafe in the shadow of old colonial buildings. The plaza, dominated by the basilica and convent of the same name, was built in the 16C. Its centerpiece, the **Fuente de los Leones** (Lions' Fountain), was carved of white Carrara marble by Italian sculptor Giuseppe Gaggini (1791-1867) and modeled after a fountain in the Alhambra Palace in Spain. Some of the commercial buildings around the plaza, such as the dome-shaped **Lonja del Comercio** (Commodity Exchange) on the north side and the **Aduana** (Customs House) on the east side, were built in the early 20C.

◆ Basilica Menor y Convento de San Francisco de Asís★★
Open Sun–Mon 9:30am–12:30pm, Tue 9:30am–5pm, Wed & Sat 9am–7pm.

This venerable set of religious buildings has endured serious hardships over the past centuries. The idea of having a Franciscan monastery in Havana took shape in 1570, but actual construction started 10 years later. Believed to have been completed around 1608, the monastery became a powerful religious center exerting a spiritual and cultural influence all over Latin America. In an advanced state of neglect, the basilica and convent were rebuilt largely in the Baroque style, beginning in 1719. In 1842, as a measure against powerful religious orders, the government of Spain confiscated the monastery, and the basilica was eventually turned into a warehouse. Four years later, a devastating hurricane destroyed its nave. Restoration work since 1990 has given the buildings a new lease on life.

Today, **concerts** featuring classical and Cuban music are held on a regular basis in the basilica *(open Fri, Sat–Sun 6pm)*. The cloister of the monastery houses a **religious museum★** *(open Mon–Sat 9:30am–4:30pm; 2CUC)* displaying artifacts and furniture as well as the 16C ceramic and glass remnants found during excavations on-site.

◗ *Walk south towards the docks, and turn left on Calle Sol.*

Plaza de San Francisco de Asís

©Claire Boobbyer/Michelin

You'll see a train carriage almost blocking your way. Called the **Coche Mambí** *(open Tue–Sat 9am–5:30pm, Sun 9am–1pm)*, this luxury rail car was built in the US in 1900 with bedrooms, bathrooms, a dining room and a kitchen, and was used by Cuba's presidents from 1912 to 1959. In the building opposite, you'll see silverware monogramed with the word "Mambí" and a portable ice-cream maker used by Cuba's presidents. Nearby, on the port road at no. 262 Calle San Pedro, an 18C mansion with an inner courtyard houses the **Fundación Havana Club** *(open Mon–Thu 9am–5pm, Fri–Sun 10am–4pm; 5CUC)*, a museum devoted to the history of rum-making in Cuba. After the tour, you'll get to sample rum at the tasting bar *(ground floor; open until 11pm)*. Bottles of rum can be purchased at the Havana Club Shop.

▶ *Return to the plaza and walk one block west (away from the plaza) on Calle Amargura to Calle Mercaderes.*

Take a break at the **Museo del Chocolate** *(no. 255 Calle Mercaderes; open daily 9am–9pm)*, a cafe where you can enjoy 🍫 **hot chocolate** or a cold chocolate beverage and watch the chocolate-making process.

▶ *Walk south on Calle Mercaderes to reach the final plaza (and the end of the walking tour).*

Plaza Vieja★
Constructed in the second half of the 16C, this plaza is one of the oldest squares in Havana.

Ironically, it was initially called Plaza Nueva (New Square). Plaza Vieja was built for the public at large. The slave market held here for many years was replaced with a covered market that was torn down in the early 1900s. Extensive renovation has returned the plaza to its original condition and eliminated the unsightly parking that dominated its center in the 1950s. Today this cobbled square, surrounded by restored historic houses and mansions, has a new marble fountain as well.

♦ Casa de las Hermanas Cárdenas
This small ochre-colored house *(corner of Brasil and San Ignacio)* was built for the Cárdenas sisters in the late 18C. It became the headquarters of the Havana Philharmonic Society in 1924. Today the **Centro de Desarollo de las Artes Visuales** (Center for the Development of Visual Arts) hosts temporary exhibits of contemporary art on the premises *(open Tue–Sat 10am–4pm)*. Almost right across the street, the blue house called the **Casa de Esteban José Portier** (1752) is home to the **Fototeca de Cuba** *(open Tue–Sat 10am–3pm)*, which organizes photo exhibits in its lovely patio. Note the fine Mudejar woodwork inside the house. Next to the Fototeca stands the new planetarium, the latest edition to Old Havana's attractions.

♦ Planetario
Plaza Vieja. (7) 864 9165. 10CUC. Reservations in person or by phone Mon–Tue 9:30am–3:30pm for shows Wed–Sun 10am, 11am, 12:30pm and 3.30pm. Spanish guide only.

Plaza Vieja

©Sylvaine Poitau/Apa Publications

A huge fiberglass sun, surrounded by the planets, greets visitors to the Old Town's planetarium. Interactive displays *(ground floor)* indictate people's weight and age if they stepped on Mars, Saturn or the moon. An astronomer explains the universe before a simulated Big Bang explosion occurs under a glass-floor panel beneath the sun installation. Inside the sun is an auditorium. Here the night sky is beamed across the dome to the sound of relaxing music and an explanation of constellations before the sun rises in the east and the night sky, filled with stars, disappears on the other side.

◗ *Walk clockwise for a surprising find on the southeast corner of the plaza.*

The former **Hotel Palacio Viena** (1906), an Art Nouveau gem, also known as Palacio Cueto, is finally being brought back to life thanks to a joint restoration effort by Cuba and Austria.
The **Casa del Conde de Jaruco★** *(southwest corner of San Ignacio and Muralla)* is perhaps the most remarkable architecture on the plaza. It was built in 1737, but multiple alterations were subsequently made. Damaged over the years, the old mansion was restored, and now houses La Casona art gallery and the **Fondo Cubano de Bienes Culturales**, which stages art exhibits and sells handicrafts. Admire its beautiful façade and charming **inner courtyard★**.

A Cluster of Convents
Southwest of Plaza Vieja, in the vicinity of Calle Cuba, which parallels Calle San Ignacio, are three convents and two churches that are worth seeing.

Convento de Santa Clara★★
Open daily 9am–5pm. 2CUC. Renovation ongoing.
Santa Clara was the first nunnery on the island. Construction of the Franciscan convent was completed in 1644. The loss of privacy due to new construction around the religious community prompted it to move out in 1919. Later the property became the offices of the Ministry of Public Works. Today it is home to the National Center of Conservation, Restoration

Convento de Santa Clara
©Claire Boobbyer/Michelin

hall where old furniture and religious artifacts are restored. The main **cloister★★** reveals a handsome tile roof and porticoed stone galleries around a central courtyard. Palm trees, ceibas, yagrumas and other plants provide a graceful setting for its centerpiece: the first public fountain in Havana, the 17C **Fuente de la Samaritana**. The nuns' cells were converted into workshops where textiles, furniture, paintings and statues are repaired and restored. Some of the cells have kept their original, elaborate **woodwork★** dating to the mid-17C. Peek inside the church to see its rectangular nave and remarkable ceiling. The adjoining cloisters have been turned into the **Residencia Académica Convento de Santa Clara**, a residence hall for university students (particularly those majoring in art restoration). Travelers are also welcome to stay, provided there is vacancy *(see Hotels)*.

and Museology, dedicated to preserving Cuba's cultural patrimony. With limited means, its staff restores precious artworks. Begun in 1982, painstaking work to restore Santa Clara continues today. Every building has been renovated except the third cloister. Ask for a guide to show you the

Iglesia del Espíritu Santo

The oldest church still standing in Havana is located on the same street, at the corner of Calle Acosta. This rather stern-looking edifice was built in 1632 by free slaves. At that time, there was just one other church in Havana: the structure (c. 1550) that stood on the site of the Palacio de los Capitanes Generales before the palacio's construction. The left nave and façade were added to the "Church of the Holy Spirit" in the second half of the 18C.

Iglesia de Nuestra Señora de la Merced
©Claire Boobbyer/Michelin

Iglesia y Convento de Nuestra Señora de la Merced★

Two blocks south on Calle Cuba *(at Calle Merced)*, this three-nave church, begun in 1755, boasts a white façade with six pillars as well as late-Italian Baroque and early Neoclassical elements.

As you step inside, note the central cupola decorated with **frescoes★**, the **sacristy furniture★**, and the relics on display in the crypt. Visit the peaceful cloister to find a respite from the heat.

▷ *Continue south on Calle Cuba, and at the next intersection, turn left onto Calle Leonor Pérez (Paula).*

Iglesia de San Francisco de Paula★

This unusual church stands on a small plaza overlooking the bay. Its octagonal **dome★** and elaborate Baroque façade are all that remain of a former church and women's hospital built in the late 1660s. A hurricane that swept the island in 1730 severely damaged both structures, necessitati g rebuilding.

By 1946, the long-abandoned buildings were so dilapidated that the old hospital was razed, while most of the church was fortunately spared. Under the auspices of the City Historian's Office, the church *(closed for repairs)* has now become a concert venue for **Ars Longa**, a Cuban music ensemble that plays medieval and baroque compositions here *(Fri–Sun 6pm)*.

▷ *Return to Calle Cuba and continue north to Espíritu Santo. Turn left onto Calle Acosta and go three blocks.*

On Calle Acosta, you'll see a Baroque-style arched walkway called **Arco de Belén** (Arch of Bethlehem). The arch was built in 1772 to link the Church and Convent of Our Lady of Bethlehem *(see below)* to buildings that had been purchased across the street to enlarge the property.

▷ *At the Arch of Bethlehem, turn right on Calle Compostela.*

Iglesia y Convento de Nuestra Señora de Belén★
Open Mon–Fri 8am–4pm.

This large complex, completed in 1718 for the Order of Bethlehem, was the first example of Baroque architecture in Havana. In 1042 the religious community was expelled, and the property was confiscated by the Spanish government. In 1856 it was turned over to the Jesuits, who founded a preparatory school for the elite called **Real Colegio de Belén** (Royal College of Bethlehem) in the convent. An **observatory** (Observatorio Real) was built in 1858 for the purpose of weather prediction, and one of its directors, a Spanish Jesuit priest named Father **Benito Viñes** (1837–1893), actually laid the foundation for the science of hurricane forecasting. Its student population growing, the Jesuit school moved to the Marianao district in 1925. The abandoned church and convent fell into disrepair, further damaged by fire in 1991. After painstaking restorations led by the City Historian's Office, the buildings are again dedicated to charitable uses (a home for senior citizens and center for disabled children).

CENTRO HABANA

Stretching west of Old Havana, Centro Habana is bounded on the north by the Malecón, on the west by Cazalda da Infante, and on the east by Paseo del Prado (also known as Paseo de Martí).

On its easternmost side, Centro, as it is simply known, boasts its most glorious landmark, the Capitolio Nacional, from which extends the attractive Prado, the dividing line between Centro and Old Havana. A historic theater and two prominent parks flank the Prado near the Capitolio. Yet much of the central part of the city is rundown. The locals sometimes refer to the area—the capital's most densely populated neighborhood—as Beirut or Baghdad, because of its ramshackle buildings, gaping holes in the sidewalks and a general air of decrepitude. The urban renaissance taking place in La Habana Vieja hasn't spread to Centro Habana, although it has started, most notably along the Malecón. But tourists who avoid exploring this area risk missing a fascinating aspect of Cuban life as it is lived by the city's plumbers, hairstylists, dressmakers and other residents who make their homes here. Two especially colorful areas are worth seeing: Havana's Chinatown (Barrio Chino) and the Callejón de Hamel. No visit to Havana is complete without a stroll along the Malecón.

✸ Walking Tour

⛄ The Malecón★★

One of the capital city's most cherished landmarks, the **Malecón** is affectionately called *El gran sofa* ("the big sofa") by the locals. All year long hundreds of residents and tourists come here night and day to while away the hours sitting on its **seawall** and taking in the scenery. The wide waterfront **boulevard** extends about 8km/5mi on Havana's northern shore, from the Castillo de San Salvador de la Punta in La Habana Vieja west to the Almendares River, which separates Vedado from Miramar. The pedestrian **sidewalk** that was built next to the six-lane coastal thoroughfare offers a microcosm of life in Havana.

The Malecón

© Hervé Hughes/hemis.fr

Here youngsters scamper up the seawall, anglers watch their lines, vendors sell cheap cigars, lovers recline entwined, and men yell out compliments to female passers-by, as vintage American cars and coco-taxis cruise Havana's busiest east-west street.

Sunset casts an array of vivid colors on the rows of 19C and early 20C balconied buildings that line the Malecón in its Centro Habana's portion. In stormy weather, the walkway is empty, as heavy winds send waves crashing over the seawall, flooding the road and spraying the weather-beaten buildings with corrosive salt from the ocean waters.

▷ *Access the Prado (Paseo de Martí) from the Malecón and walk south.*

The Prado★

One of the city's most attractive and popular promenades, this broad, tree-lined thoroughfare (also named Paseo de Martí) divides Centro Habana from La Habana Vieja. It is paved in marble and dotted with marble benches. Once the haunt of the aristocracy,

Touring Tip

There is a significant police presence in **Centro Habana**, and although most tourists will never encounter any problems, keep in mind that this is a rather seedy part of town and take common-sense precautions: don't carry a lot of cash, don't wear expensive jewels, and avoid side streets at night, especially if you are alone.

the Prado Is now frequented mostly by seniors taking a siesta and children playing or skating. The buildings flanking the street sport varied styles, some heavy with rococo decoration, but all showing signs of age.

The avenue down the center is graced with splendid wrought-iron street lights.

▷ *Continue south on the Prado to reach the Capitolio Nacional.*

Capitolio Nacional★★
Closed for renovation.

One of Havana's great landmarks *(see Cuban Classics)*, this 200m/656ft-long replica of the US Capitol

The Prado

©Clare Boobbyer/Michelin

DISTRICTS

55

HOTELS

Alejandro Martinez	①	Casa 1932 ③	Presidente ⑪
Amparo Lopez	⑤	Deauville ④	Zoyla Zayas Ulloa ⑫
Armando y Betty Gutiérez	⑥	TRYP Habana Libre ⑦	Silvia Vidal ⑬
Casa Alicia	②	Iliana García ⑨	Victoria ⑧
		Nacional (Hotel) ⑩	

A   B

1

Malecón
CVD
José Martí
Casa de las
Américas
⑪ Calzada
Museo de
la Danza
Línea
Miramar
Línea
Hubert
de Blanck
⑦ T
VEDADO
Avenida de los Presidentes
Memorial a las Víctimas
del Maine
Caleta
Nacional
⑤ ② B
T
Guiñol
Focsa
Banco Nacional
de Cuba
Torreón de
San Lázaro
⑨ ⑧ ⑥ ⑤
Rampa
Hospital
Príncipe
Vapor
Coppelia
TRYP
Habana Libre
⑧ ⑦
25
27 de Noviembre (Jovellar)
Callejón
de Hamel
Soledad
Aramburu

2

Museo de
Artes
Decorativas ③
El Sótano T
Universidad
de La Habana
Museo Montané
Monumento
José A. Mella
Museo
Napoleónico
Calzada de Infanta
San Francisco
Espada
Hospital
Museo
José Miguel
Gómez
Juan
Abrahantes
Zapata
Zanja
Salud
Castillejo
Paseo
27
E
Castillo
del Príncipe
29
Quinta
de los Molinos
Avenida Salvador Allende (Carlos III)
Plasencia
Retiro
Sitios
PLAZA
DE LA REVOLUCIÓN
⑨ ⑬
⑩
Calzada de
Zapata
Feria
de la
Juventud
Pozos Dulces
Bruzón
Desagüe
Lugareño
Almendra
Calzada de Ayestarán
Calzada de Infanta

3

① ①
Teatro
Nacional
35
Cementerio de
Cristóbal Colón
⑭
Ministerio
del Interior
Memorial
José Martí
Plaza de la
Revolución
Palacio
de la Revolución
Avenida de Colón
Bellavista
Panorama
Hidalgo
Loma
Lombillo
NUEVO VEDADO
Conill
Tulipán
Ermita
San Pedro
Ministerio de
Comunicaciones
Biblioteca
Nacional
Aranguren
(Zaldo)
San Martin
Ave. 20 de Mayo
Panchito Gómez
Masón
Gral. E. Núñez
Pancho Pérez
Auditor
Estadio
Latinoamericano
Quinta
de los Condes
de Santovenia
EL CERRO
Amenidad
Pedroso
Zequeira
Patria
Calzada del Cerro
Fábrica Bocoy

RESTAURANTS

Amigos (Los)	⑥	Cafe Laurent ⑤	Guardia (La) ④
Asahi	①	Casona de 17 (La) ②	Monguito ⑧
Atelier	⑦	Gringo Viejo (El) ③	Nerei ⑨
		Castropol ⑪	Rampa (La) ⑫

✈ Parque Lenin

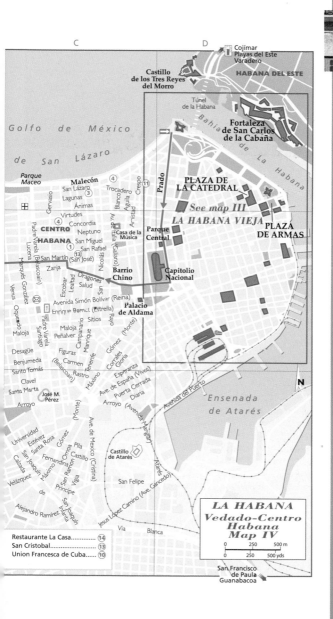

Restaurante La Casa.............. ⑭
San Cristobal........................ ⑬
Union Francesca de Cuba...... ⑩

LA HABANA
Vedado–Centro
Habana
Map IV

0   250   500 m
0   250   500 yds

Capitolio Nacional

©Claire Boobbyer/Michelin

Building in Washington, DC, was home to Cuba's legislature for many years, and now houses the Ministry of Science, Technology and the Environment.

To its north lies **Parque Central**, and to its south stretches vast **Parque de la Fraternidad**, both nearly always full of people *(see Parks And Gardens)*.

Opposite Parque Central sits one of Havana's important cultural venues, the **Gran Teatro de La Habana★★** *(see Cuban Classics)*.

Behind the Capitolio, **Fábrica de Tabacos Partagás★**, at no. 520 Calle Industria, is one of Cuba's oldest cigar factories *(open Mon–Fri 9am–11am and noon–2:45pm; 45min guided tour 10CUC; buy ticket in Hotel Saratoga)*.

Guided tours explore stages of the cigar-making process. Afterwards, step inside the factory store where there's a selection of tobacco for sale.

◐ *Just south of the cigar factory, follow Calle Dragones west to Calle Amistad.*

Barrio Chino (Chinatown)

Just beyond the corner of Calles Dragones and Amistad, a large **Chinese gateway**, called *paifang*, marks the entrance to Chinatown. The first half of the 19C saw successive slave rebellions in Cuba. To make up for a labor shortage, thousands of Chinese indentured servants (those contracted to work for a fixed period of time) were brought in from Guangdong Province, Hong Kong, Macau and Taiwan beginning in 1847. After fulfilling their contracts, some of them settled permanently in Havana. They opened grocery stores, restaurants, laundries, pharmacies and other small family businesses. In the second half of the 19C, thousands more Chinese came to Cuba from California, fleeing anti-Chinese sentiment there. In its heyday, Havana's Chinatown occupied 44 square blocks and was the largest Chinese enclave in Latin America, with a population upwards of 120,000 people. But when Fidel Castro took over the country in 1959 and nationalized privately owned businesses, many

Hamel's Hero

Salvador González Escalona, a self-taught Afro-Cuban painter and sculptor, was deeply inspired by Picasso, Dalí, Gaudí and Hundertwasser.

The spiritual influence of Santería—the syncretic religion that blends traditional West African religion brought by slaves to Cuba with Roman Catholicism *(see sidebar p39)*—is also evident in his work, a kitschy mix of cubism, expressionism, surrealism and the primitive style.

The artist not only paints trompe-l'œil and inspirational messages on walls and canvas, he also uses scrap objects to make clever Duchampian sculptures, and won't hesitate to pour old bathtubs with concrete to transform them into public benches.

A black Mercury parked on the alley usually means that the maestro is home. So go on in and visit his grotto-like studio and gallery where his works are for sale.

Chinese Cubans fled, and the once-thriving community started to dwindle. Today, it is bounded by **Calle Zanja** to the north and **Avenida Simón Bolívar** (Reina) to the south. A highlight of the neighborhood is **El Cuchillo de Zanja**, the pedestrian street decorated with red lanterns and paper dragons, where several Chinese restaurants are located. Don't miss the *agromercado*, a little farmers' market at the corner of Calle Zanja and Calle Rayo, where vendors sell Chinese-Cuban food that blends Asian and Caribbean flavors. A newspaper is published in Chinese here twice a week, and Chinese New Year is celebrated annually with fireworks and a traditional dragon parade.

○ *Walk west approximately 10 blocks to Calle Aramburu, turn right onto Aramburu and walk north.*

Callejón de Hamel★
Between Calle Aramburu and Calle Hospital on Hamel, just south of San Lázaro.

The Callejón de Hamel (Hamel's Alley) is located in **Cayo Hueso**, a drab corner of Centro Havana with more than its share of decaying buildings. Back in 1990 **Salvador González Escalona** (b.1948) *(see sidebar above)* began to transform a run-down neighborhood into the dazzling, pyrotechnic explosion of color, music and hope that it has become today. He painted a mural on a friend's house to brighten it up. Reactions were so overwhelmingly positive that, with the neighbors' blessings, he covered each wall within **two full blocks** with his bright motifs.

Every Sunday at noon, the Callejón de Hamel hosts a legendary **rumba street party** to honor the deities of the *Santería* religion. The entire neighborhood is packed with musicians, dancers, locals and tourists. It's an occasion to treat yourself to a cocktail called *negrón*, a potent mix of rum, lemon, honey and basil served at **El Negrón**, a local joint with some intriguing aphorisms painted on its red walls, such as: "Fishes don't know water exists."

DISTRICTS

59

VEDADO★

West of Centro Habana lies the Plaza de la Revolución *municipio*. Within this district, north of the Cementerio de Cristóbal Colón (Christopher Columbus Cemetery), the popular Vedado neighborhood, which extends west to the Almendares River, makes up the more modern and active heart of Havana. Lying south of Vedado, Nuevo Vedado is largely a residential zone.

The University of Havana is here, and so are several museums. **Nuevo Vedado** is a residential area south of the cemetery. Many hotels, restaurants, *paladares* and other businesses catering to tourists, such as airline companies and travel agencies, are located around La Rampa, the main commercial artery of the capital. Cigar-sellers, *jineteras (see sidebar p125)* and taxi drivers seem more numerous here than elsewhere in Havana. Their favorite hangouts

are at hotel entrances, where they offer their services to tourists. The "pssst" sound that they make to passers-by is the traditional Cuban way of getting your attention. Just say no politely yet firmly and you'll find that these eager vendors don't have much perseverance.

La Rampa★ (Calle 23)

Calle 23 runs more than 2km/1mi through Vedado, from the Malecón southwest to the Columbus cemetery. Known as the Rampa along the stretch between the Hotel Nacional and Hotel Tryp Habana Libre, the thoroughfare is lined with travel agencies, airline offices and banks. Lively day and night, the Rampa hums during business hours with commercial activity that gives way to the

Touring Tip

Sights in Vedado are quite spread out, so it's best to get around by taxi or **coco-taxi**. Allow at least a day for your visit, more for a walking tour.

Hotel Nacional

©Sylvaine Poitau/Apa Publications

MUST SEE

frenetic nightlife of hotel bars and discotheques during off-hours.

Hotel Nacional★

At the lower entrance to the Rampa rises the handsome Art Deco silhouette of this landmark hotel, an imposing multistory building perched atop a promontory *(see Cuban Classics)*. Many celebrities have availed themselves of the Nacional's accommodations since it was built in the 1930s. Enjoy a mojito on the terrace, which is ideally situated for taking in expansive views of Havana Bay.

Monument to the Victims of USS Maine

Behind the Hotel Nacional, at the corner of Malecón and Avenida 19, looms this double-columned monument. The ship was an armored cruiser that exploded suddenly and sank in Havana harbor on February 15, 1898, precipitating the Spanish-American War. Scraps from the vessel are on view nearby, and the monument itself bears the names of those who perished in the explosion. The memorial, which was erected in 1925 to celebrate Cuban-American relations, was partially destroyed by a hurricane the following year. After the Revolution, a bronze eagle and busts of American presidents were removed from the monument to protest US policies toward Cuba.

Edificio Focsa

Two blocks west of the Rampa rises Havana's tallest skyscraper. The square-shaped tower at the corner of Calle 17 and M boasts a bar-restaurant on the top floor; head on up to take in the incomparable **view★★★** of Havana.

Hotel TRYP Habana Libre

Symbol of the Rampa, this hotel, formerly the Havana Hilton, was completed in 1957 to welcome American tourists who flooded Cuba. Following the Revolution the hotel was nationalized. It makes an excellent reference point for orienting yourself within Vedado.

Coppelia★

Calle 23 and Calle L. Open Tue–Sun 10am–9:15pm. (7) 832 6184. Diagonally opposite TRYP Habana Libre hotel, at the intersection of Calle L, a curious rounded structure occupies the center of a pleasant square. This building

---

Getting Oriented in Vedado

See Map pp 56-57. The street layout in Vedado [pronounced beh-dar-doh] mirrors the regular grid pattern of Centro Habana. It's easy to find your way around, thanks to the street-numbering system posted on signs at each intersection. Streets running southwest to northeast are marked with odd numbers that increase from the Malecón to the Plaza de la Revolución. The perpendicular streets are marked alphabetically from A to P from east of Paseo to the waterfront, then with even numbers to the Almendares River. Skyscrapers in the district can serve as reference points; the TRYP Habana Libre hotel rises above La Rampa, and the Hotel Meliá Cohiba sits at the foot of Paseo.

A Bourgeois Neighborhood Evolves

Until the last century, building construction was not permitted in Vedado (the word means, literally, "forbidden") in order to preserve an unobstructed view of the sea in case of attack. But as wealthy Cuban tycoons left the popular eastern neighborhoods around the beginning of the 20C, they built grand mansions here, creating a residential zone. Luxury hotels and casinos followed, and the area flourished with fast and loose distractions that attracted a burgeoning tourism industry through the 1950s. Several decades later, it remains a popular entertainment area full of bars and clubs. New buildings continue to spring up here and there in the district, even as some of the once-elegant villas fall into disrepair due to the ravages of Cuba's climate and poor economy.

houses an ⛄ **ice cream parlor** that is a veritable social institution in Havana, immortalized in the 1994 film *Fresa y Chocolate* (Strawberry and Chocolate). The title is something of a misnomer since quite often the only flavor available is vanilla. Regardless, you'll find *habaneros* lining up to wait for hours for a serving of Coppelia's ice cream. If you don't want to wait in line, you can purchase Coppelia ice cream at a small sit-down side section in exchange for CUCs.

Hilltop Homage

To reach the university from the Rampa, take Calle L southeast from the Hotel Tryp Habana Libre to its intersection with Avenida 27.

Universidad de La Habana
The University of Havana was moved to this hilltop site from Old Havana in 1902. At the bottom of an enormous staircase leading to the university buildings, you'll find a monument honoring José Mella. One of the founders of the Cuban Communist Party, Mella was assassinated in 1929. Behind the Neoclassical façade of the building lies a small, verdant park where students gather to study.

On the university campus, the **Museo Antropológico Montané** *(open Mon–Sat 9am–noon and 1pm–4pm; 1CUC)* presents ⛄ **artifacts** of pre-Columbian civilizations, including a wooden phallic-shaped tobacco idol. Behind the university campus rises the magnificently restored **Museo Napoleónico★**, a Florentine-style palace housing one of the

Vase, Museo Napoleónico

©Claire Boobbyer/Michelin

world's most extensive collections of Napoleon artifacts and memorabilia *(see Museums)*.

Castillo del Príncipe

South of the university, on the other side of Calle G (Avenida de los Presidentes), several medical facilities surround a hill. Pass the Hospital Ortopédico to get to this fortress. It was erected in 1779 as a military prison and observation post from which Havana's defenders could spot invaders from afar. The Castillo is now a military zone with no public access, but climb the hill to enjoy an expansive view of the city.

Vedado's Venerated

Plaza de la Revolución

This immense esplanade *(see Revolutionary Sites)* became famous the world over because of the huge national rallies held here, when nearly a million people came to listen to Fidel Castro deliver one of his epic speeches. People still come here in the thousands on annual holidays like May 1. A number of government buildings are here, as well as the **Memorial de José Martí** and the metal sculptures of Che Guevara and Camilo Cienfuegos.

Cementerio de Cristóbal Colón★★★

End of Calle 12. Open daily 7am–5pm. 5CUC. Guided tour 1CUC. Located west of Plaza de la Revolución, this vast cemetery, surrounded by pale yellow walls, lies on the border between Vedado and Nuevo Vedado districts. Enter through an immense Romanesque **portico** designed by Calixto de Loira in 1870. All architectural styles can be found here, where somber gray tombs stand next to richly ornate monuments. Some of Cuba's most prominent political and cultural personalities are interred in this cemetery.
The city of the dead is laid out in perfect grid formation, and the Neo-Byzantine Central Chapel serves as a good reference point

©Claire Boobbyer/Michelin

Cementerio de Cristóbal Colón

CEMENTERIO
DE CRISTÓBAL COLÓN

0   200 m
0   200 yds

Portada
Principal

General Máximo
Gómez Báez

Alejo
Carpentier

Galería de
Tobías

Plaza N.O.

Escultura de
Rita Longa

Plaza
Cristóbal
Colón

Plaza N.E.

Carlos
J. Finlay Barres

Réplica de la Obra
la Piedad de Miguel Ángel

Monumento
A los Bomberos

Estudiantes
de Medicina

La Milagrosa

Hubert
de Blanck

Falla-
Bonet

Cecilia Valdés

Puerta Oeste

Fray
Jacinto

Cirilo
Villaverde

Veteranos de las Guerras
de Independencia

Capilla
central

Ave. Obispo

Puerta
Este

Colonia Francesa
de Cuba

Martires del Asalto
al Palacio Presidencial

Loma Julia Borges

Panteón de Las Fuerzas
Armadas Revolucionarias

San Antonio Chiquito

Puerta Sur

Ave. de Colón

Calzada de Zapata

N

for getting your bearings. The chapel's 19C **fresco** is the work of Cuban painter Miguel Melero. Noteworthy monuments include the hard-to-miss **Monumento a los Bomberos** (main pathway), a huge sculpture dedicated to the 28 firemen who lost their lives in the fire of May 17, 1890.

The monument features the figures of the Angel of Death, torch in hand, and of a nun with a pelican at her feet.

The tomb of Doña Amelia de Gloria Castellano Pérez, nicknamed **La Milagrosa** (The Miraculous One), is a popular point of pilgrimage. As the story goes, when the tomb was opened the skeleton of Doña Amelia's child was found in her arms, although upon burial the child had been laid at its mother's feet. Since this discovery, pilgrims have visited the spot, leaving flowers and praying for Doña Amelia's aid.

The tomb of composer **Hubert De Blanck** bears a domino with double threes, evoking the game De Blanck was playing when he died.

The tomb of Cuban novelist **Alejo Carpentier** is here as well as that of 19C author **Cirilo Villaverde**, which lies not far from the resting place of Cecilia Valdés, the mulatta heroine of Villaverde's most famous novel of the same name, *Cecilia Valdés* (1882).

Other highlights include the **angel doors** of the Catalina-Lasa Baró Art-Deco mausoleum, the Art Deco Rita Longa **sculpture** inside the Aguilera tomb, and the **gold mural** by René Portocarrero inside the tomb of the Familía Raúl de Zárraga at Avenida Obispo Fray Jacinto and Calle 5.

MIRAMAR★

One of Havana's 15 municipalities, the Playa municipio begins west of Vedado, beyond the mouth of the Río Almendares. This municipio contains the famed Miramar district, a fashionable residential area with exclusive hotels, restaurants and boutiques that cater to a well heeled clientele. It is known for its wide, tree-lined avenues flanked by stately mansions, many of them now home to government offices, commercial agencies, foreign corporations and most of Havana's embassies. The greenery can't conceal the crumbling sidewalks and decaying villas that have seen better days, however. Four long, busy thoroughfares run parallel to the ocean, beginning with Avenida 1, then Avenida 3 and 5, with Avenida 7 the farthest from the coast.

Making the Most of Miramar

Avenida Primera (Avenida 1)

This oceanfront avenue is not quite as pleasant and picturesque as the Malecón, but in summer, many of Havana's families find relief from the smothering heat at a scruffy little beach called **Playita del 16** *(between Calles 12 and 16)*, a far cry from Havana's inviting eastern beaches *(see Playas Del Este)*.

Quinta Avenida★ (Avenida 5)

If you are coming from Vedado, take the tunnel under the Almendares River.

Elegant Avenida 5 was originally called "Avenida de las Américas." With a decidedly American flair, it is to Havana what legendary Fifth Avenue is to New York City. One of the two architects responsible for Avenida 5 was **John H. Duncan**, who designed the General Grant National Memorial in New York City. It is also Cuba's version of Washington, DC's "Embassy Row," where most foreign diplomatic missions can be found. Stone benches dot the broad **central median** planted with bay laurel and palm trees along the avenue's 8km/5mi length.

Between Calles 24 and 26, **Parque Emiliano Zapata** honors Mexico's revolutionary hero with a statue; *jagüeyes*, wild fig trees that can reach heights of 15m/50ft, surround a charming gazebo. Fans of spy novels will want to visit the **Museo del Ministerio del Interior** *(open Tues–Sat 9am–5pm; closed Aug; 2CUC)* at the corner of Calle 14. This small, provocative museum *(displays are labeled in Spanish only)* focuses on events that have threatened Cuba's national security since Castro's arrival to power in 1960, and methods used by foreign enemies to overthrow the Cuban government.

Maqueta de La Ciudad

Calle 28, between Avenida 1 and Avenida 3. Open Mon–Fri 9:30am–5:30pm. 3CUC.

For a bird's-eye view of Havana and its layout, take a look at this huge **scale model** of the Cuban capital (22m/72ft x 10m/33ft) with streets made of colored paper and buildings of cedar wood. It indicates which renovation projects are being implemented and those that will be.

Halfway down Avenida 5, between Calles 62 and 66, you can't help but notice a sinister-looking, concrete tower from the Soviet era. It now houses the **Russian embassy**.

This recognizable landmark is clearly visible in Miramar's skyline and can help orient you if you lose your way. Just a block from the Russian diplomatic mission, at the corner of Calle 60 and Avenida 1, the tanks of the 🐠 **Acuario National de Cuba** *(open Tue–Sun 10am–10pm; 5CUC)* feature Cuba's marine fauna and flora: corals, tropical and subtropical fish, turtles, sea lions. Three dolphin shows are presented daily in a small amphitheater.

The Shops of Miramar

A few luxury boutiques and well stocked *diplomercados* can be found in Miramar. Theoretically speaking, anyone—not just foreign visitors and diplomats—should be able to shop in these state-run "dollar stores," so-called since 1993 when it became legal for Cuban citizens to own and use US dollars. But in reality, they sell food and consumer goods at prohibitive prices most locals cannot afford. The Cuban elite seem to be particularly fond of **La Maison** *(corner of Avenida 7 and Calle 1)*. In the hushed atmosphere of this stylish mansion, an attentive staff

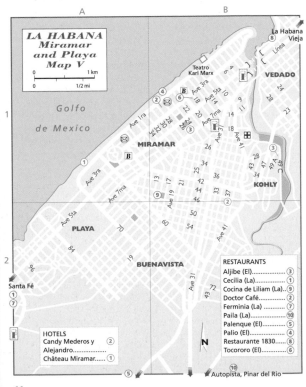

LA HABANA
*Miramar
and Playa
Map V*

0 ——— 1 km
0 ——— 1/2 mi

Golfo de Mexico

VEDADO

Teatro Karl Marx

La Habana Vieja

MIRAMAR

KOHLY

PLAYA

BUENAVISTA

Santa Fé

HOTELS
Candy Mederos y Alejandro.................. ②
Château Miramar...... ①

RESTAURANTS
Aljibe (El)..................	③
Cecilia (La)..................	①
Cocina de Liliam (La)..	⑨
Doctor Café..................	②
Ferminia (La)	⑦
Paila (La)....................	⑩
Palenque (El).............	⑤
Palio (El)....................	④
Restaurante 1830......	⑧
Tocororo (El)..............	⑥

Autopista, Pinar del Rio

MUST SEE

offers its clientele a fine selection of French perfume, jewelry, clothes and accessories. In the evening, fashion shows take place in the gardens.

Farther Afield

Continue on Avenida 5 towards Mariel Harbor. Drive past the Palacio de las Convenciones, then cross the Río Jaimanitas.

Marina Hemingway
Located in the Jaimanitas neighborhood, a 20-minute drive from the mouth of Río Almendares, this marina is dedicated to yachting, fishing and nautical sports. Not just a traditional dock equipped with basic amenities like drinking water, electricity, gas and a repair shop, it is a huge complex that encompasses hotels and restaurants, bars, stores, a swimming pool and even medical facilities. Each year, the marina organizes the **Ernest Hemingway International Blue Marlin Fishing Tournament** *(see Calendar of Events)* in honor of the great writer and avid fisherman who launched this tradition.

Touring Tip

In Miramar, **"avenidas"** or avenues have uneven numbers and intersect with "calles" or streets that have even numbers in a grid-like pattern. In this part of town, driving may be the best way to get around, since there is little traffic and the main sights are not necessarily within walking distance of one another.

Kohly District
Military barracks in this area prohibit parking. It is best to explore Kohly by bike or moped.
Part of the Playa Municipality, this district is situated southeast of Miramar, on the western banks of the Almendares River. Follow Avenida 49-C, a road running parallel to the river, and you cross this lovely residential area right by the **Bosque de La Habana**. Just a few minutes from downtown, yet tucked away from its bustle, Kohly offers peace and quiet in the middle of Havana's one and only forest.

Marina Hemingway

©Abel Ernesto/Michelin

DISTRICTS

CUBAN CLASSICS

Native architecture can hardly be said to have existed at the time of the Spanish Conquest of Cuba. In Havana the first colonial buildings were direct borrowings from the Spanish architectural tradition. Military architecture continued to follow European models. Yet other structures, such as churches and residential buildings, soon began to incorporate specifically Cuban features, reflecting the local environment and new socio-economic conditions. Havana has a magnificent heritage of buildings, from Spanish Colonial and Cuban Baroque to Neoclassical, Art Deco and beyond. The challenge is to preserve them from further decay—a challenge being addressed in La Habana Vieja at least. The buildings described below exemplify Havana's myriad architectural styles and show its urban evolution.

Catedral de San Cristóbal★★★

Empedrado and Calle San Ignacio. Open Mon–Fri 11am–2:30pm, Sat 10:30am–1pm, Sun 9:30am–12:30pm. Mass Sun 10:30am. Access to the bell tower 2CUC.

See also Districts. In the second half of the 18C, the style known as **Cuban Baroque**, an evolution of Spanish Baroque, reigned supreme. It was particularly suited to religious architecture, and Havana's cathedral, completed in 1777, is among its greatest achievements.

Restored in 1950, the cathedral was revived in 1998 for Pope John Paul II's visit. Commissioned by the Jesuits, the cathedral is made of ironstone mixed with orange coral. It displays a whole panoply of conventional Baroque features, such as pediments, volutes and niches, together with a highly individual, undulating **façade★★★** and a sinuous cornice.

Framed by asymmetrical towers, the cathedral was described by Cuban writer Alejo Carpentier as "music set in stone."

The entrance is not grand: only four shallow steps lead to a plain stone platform whose main function appears to be grounding the multiple columns. The doors, crafted of cedar and mahogany, are original.

The **interior** boast floors made of Italian marble; Cuban marble graces the steps leading to portraits embedded in niches. Simple *vitrales* (stained-glass windows) are mounted high in oval niches. Surrounded by mahogany choir stalls, the carved, low-slung **altar** is crafted of a single piece from the Carrera mines. To its left, a plaque and marble wreath mark the spot that allegedly housed Christopher Columbus' remains (thus the cathedral's name) from 1796 until their repatriation to Seville in 1898. Italian Giuseppe Perovani painted the **frescoes** high above the altar. From the cupola hangs a 2-ton bronze lamp with 244 bulbs. Tableau and paintings, some by **Jean-Baptiste Vermay** *(see Districts, El Templete)*, include one of Christopher Columbus, and a copy of the Virgin de la Caridad, Cuba's patron saint.

Instituto Superior del Arte School

© Claire Boobbyer/Michelin

Instituto Superior del Arte School★★★

1110 Calle 120, between Avenida 9 and Avenida 13. Cubanacán. Playa. Visit by appointment only, Departamento de Comunicación (7) 208 9771.

The National Arts School, known as ISA for short, was one of the first commissioned projects of the new Revolution. It was built on golf club land in the Country Club district, which is now called Cubanacán, lying southwest of Miramar. Three architects—Cuban-born Ricardo Porro, and Italian-born Vittorio Garatti and Roberto Gottardi— worked on the project from 1962 to 1965, building schools of dance, *artes plasticas*, music, ballet and *arte esenica* (including theater). Due to economic conditions, the project was not completed. Work commenced on restoration in 1999, following meetings in Havana with all three architects, but the process has been slow. The only restored complex is the School of Artes Plasticas. Work has been undertaken to prevent deterioration.

Today the prestigious institution offers classes to talented local and international students in Cuban art, dance, theater, audiovisual media, and music.
Brick is the principal material used, since steel and concrete were in short supply when the project began. Constructed according to the *tabicada* tradition of Spain's Catalonia region, each building is distinguished by a series of **Catalan vaults and domes**. Clad in terra-cotta tiles, the domed enclosures are connected by winding covered walkways, also of brick. The result is an organic, undulating form that unifies the complex and creates an appearance of primitivism. Much comment is made about the sexual symbolism of the architecture, best exemplified by a **brick fountain**, whose shape suggests a vagina, perched on the edge of a pond.

Capitolio Nacional★★

Closed for three years for repairs.

Completed in 1928, Cuba's 210m/692ft-long capitol building bears a striking resemblance to

69

the US Capitol in Washington, DC. Home to the country's government for many years, it is now a major tourist attraction housing the Ministry of Science, Technology and the Environment. The monumental structure richly embodies the **Neoclassical style**, since the US Capitol building itself was modeled after the Classical-style Pantheon in Rome. Stairs lead up to a portico entrance with two rows of granite columns topped by Ionic capitals. Crowned with a cupola, the dome rises nearly 92m/300ft.

The main entrance leads directly into the main hall **rotunda**, where a 49-ton gilded bronze **statue** by sculptor Angelo Zanelli represents the Republic. At the center of the main hall, a diamond is embedded in the floor; the gem marks Cuba's Kilometer Zero, and it is from this point that all distances in Cuba are calculated. The enormous **Salón de los Pasos Perdidos** (Hall of Lost Steps)—so named for its exceptional acoustics—leads to the various rooms within the

capitol. Among the main-floor meeting rooms and offices, the semicircular room is the place where Cuban legislators met. Beautiful frescos decorate the walls and ceiling of the **Salón Martí**. Fine, rare woods grace the **Library of Science and Technology**★.

Gran Teatro de La Habana★★

Between Calles San José and San Rafael. Open Mon–Fri 9am–5pm. Guided tour 2CUC.

Looming over the Prado, the Great Theater of Havana sports an imposing **Neo-Baroque façade** designed with rounded ground-floor arches *(portales)*, and embellished with balustrades, statues and balconies in white marble. From the double-tiered tower on each corner, a statue of an angel appears poised to take flight. The present structure was designed by Belgian architect Paul Delau as an annex to the original 19C Teatro Tacón (now incorporated into the building) and

Capitolio's dome and Gran Teatro's façade

© Patrick Escudero/hemis.fr

MUST SEE

served as home to the Galicians' social club. The prominent building was completed in 1915 by the same construction firm that built the adjacent Capitolio, as well as the Centro Asturiano (now part of the Museo Nacional de Bellas Artes) that the theater faces across Parque Central.

Today the building is best known for its association with Cuba's national ballet and serves as the primary venue for Havana's International Ballet Festival. A handsome marble **staircase** rises to the second floor, winding around a beautiful mosaic on the ground floor. Dance rehearsals on the main stage are open to the public on weekdays. Operas and concerts are held in the evenings, as are performances of the Ballet Nacional de Cuba, which is still under the direction of prima ballerina **Alicia Alonso**, a noteworthy cultural figure of the Cuban Revolution.

Hotel Sevilla★★

55 Trocadero.
www.accorhotels.com.

This historic Old Havana hotel, now owned by the Mercure group, shows off an exotic façade recently renovated in vivid mustard-yellow that is decidedly **Neo-Moorish**. This style is confined to the central entry and the three floors above it. Ogee arches grace each side of the entrance. The second floor has squat columns and balustraded balconies. Flanked by pilasters, the unified third and fourth-floor façade features double-stacked balustraded balconies, elaborated-ogee windows, and a trefoil-arch window on each side. Two floors

Hotel Sevilla

©Claire Boobbyer/Michelin

of the exterior entry are clad in a diamond-shaped pattern that lends richness to the surface, as do the muted hues of ochre and blue and pink pastels. Both sides of the central entry boast shuttered balconies with curved white wrought-iron balustrades. An adjoining building continues up nine stories; its pink-colored exterior is plain in contrast. Erected in 1908, the Gran Hotel Sevilla was the Prado's tallest building in the area of the Capitolio. Designed in the Moorish style by Antonio and Rogelio Rodríguez, it became a magnet for Cuba's high society, international celebrities, and even gangsters like Al Capone and Santos Traficante. American tourists appreciated its telephones, electric lights and private bathrooms, all luxuries at the time. In 1917 an extension was added and the hotel was operated by Americans as the Hotel Sevilla Biltmore.

The spacious lobby of the 178-room hotel is trimmed in dark

71

wood, and features square columns with patterned Andalucian tiles at the base. An 8m/26ft long reception counter, covered with the same Moorish tiles, stretches one-third the length of the room. *See also Hotels.*

Coppelia★

Calle 23 (La Rampa) at the intersection of Calle L. Open Tue–Sun 10am–9:15pm.

This large, rounded structure made of glass and concrete sits within a pleasant square along La Rampa. It houses the main outlet of a Havana institution, the state-run Coppelia ice-cream parlors. Occupying one full block, the two-story building was designed in the **Modern style** by Mario Girona in 1966. Resembling a space ship, it recalls the futuristic appearance of Los Angeles International Airport's 1961 theme building.

The roof forms a circular pavilion topped by a small central turret.

Long concrete beams, or girders, reach out from the roof and arch to the ground at intervals, dividing the outdoor space into patios, where customers sit at tables to enjoy the flavor of the day. The indoor dining space on both floors is lined with windows that flood the interior with light.

Edificio Bacardí★

Corner of Monserrate and San Juan de Dios. Open during office hours.

Rising two blocks east of the Prado, this stylish 6-story building stands out among its neighbors in La Habana Vieja. Now an archetype in **Art Deco's** international vocabulary, it was built in 1930 for Emilio Bacardí, a wealthy sugarcane plantation owner and founder of the famed brand of Bacardi rum. The building's ochre-colored façade exhibits the linear symmetry and ceramic ornamentation associated with Art Deco; the roofline and central tower are especially rich in terracotta detailing. The figure of a bat at the top of the tower is the mascot that appears on the label of Bacardi products. The stylized nymphs on the tiles flanking the top three windows are said to be the work of Maxfield Parrish. Awash in pastels—another hallmark of the Deco style—the **interior** boasts marble floors and wrought-iron features.

Edificio Bacardi

© Hervé Hughes/hemis.fr

Hotel Nacional★

Calle 21 and Calle O. www.hotelnacionaldecuba.com.

At the seaside entrance to La Rampa in Vedado, this historic 8-story hotel dominates a

MUST SEE

promontory overlooking the Straits of Florida. Its massive silhouette remains a familiar landmark in Havana's skyline.

Edged with tall Royal palm trees, a long driveway leads to the hotel's entrance. American architectural firm McKim, Mead and White designed the 450-room hotel with the clean vertical lines that typify Art Deco, but added Spanish-Moorish and Neoclassical elements to give the building an overall **eclectic style**. The Neoclassical portico, crowned with a balustrade, opens in a wide rounded arch supported by Doric columns and edged with quoins. Aligned with the building's protruding wings, twin turrets dominate the roof, each turret cornered by cupolas. Since opening in December 1930, the hotel has hosted a number of well-known international guests over the years, including prime ministers, governors, movie stars, Nobel Prize winners and sports figures. Photos of the hotel's celebrity guests are displayed today in the Bay View Bar, nicknamed the Hall of Fame. Every December the hotel hosts the renowned Latin American Film Festival *(see Calendar of Events)*.

Teatro América

253 Calle Galiano, at the corner of Calle Concordia.

This theater sits on the ground floor of an enormous chalk-white Art-Deco apartment building on Avenida de Italia—Centro Habana's main thoroughfare, commonly known as Galiano. Fronted by a neon Art-Deco sign reading "AMERICA," the building was constructed in 1941 by architects Fernando Martínez Campos and Pascual de Rojas as the Rodríguez Vázquez apartment block.

Modern glass doors open into the foyer, which is flanked by two symmetrical staircases. Notice the black and cream terrazzo floor inlaid with a circular zodiac calendar and symbols. The highlight of the interior is the **ladies' cloakroom★★**, framed by a curving staircase whose baluster features wrought-iron Art-Deco ornamentation. The spacious cloakroom is appointed with mint-green paneled walls, a terrazzo floor, wrought-iron lamps, and Art-Deco chairs and sofas in duck-egg blue. The men's cloakroom is also dramatic with its chocolate-brown leather wall paneling, an Art Deco lamp and a frieze depicting athletes. The intimate theater hall itself rises to a semi-circular dome and is lined with tiered, curvilinear balconies equipped with bulbous box seats.

©Claire Boobbyer/Michelin

Ladies' cloakroom, Teatro América

SPANISH FORTS

Havana is blessed with a superb, capacious harbor—its greatest natural asset—and the conquering Spaniards knew it. By 1540 they had erected a makeshift fortress on the west side of Havana Bay to guard the harbor. Although this stronghold sustained several pirate attacks, it did not prevent the town from being pillaged and burned. Eventually a new, stronger fort, Castillo de la Real Fuerza, was built to replace it. Three more strongholds were constructed—on each side of the mouth of the harbor and across the bay, opposite Castillo de la Real Fuerza. Still standing today, these massive fortifications are a major attraction, especially for historians and military buffs.

Castillo de la Real Fuerza★

Avnenida Carlos Manuel de Céspedes, between Calle O'Reilly and Empedrado, next to Plaza de Armas. Open Mon–Sat 9am–6pm. 1CUC.

Overlooking Havana Bay, the city's first stone fort dominates the grounds along Avenida del Puerto just north of Plaza de Armas. One of a series of coastal bastions built around the island for defense against pirates and European enemies, it is reputedly the oldest fortification in the Americas. This "Castle of the Royal Force" was commissioned by the Spanish king in 1558, not long after a vicious attack on Havana by French pirate Jacques de Sores, in 1555. The new fort was completed in 1577. Over the years it housed the island's

Spanish governors, and later various national entities, before becoming a museum. Constructed of limestone, the squat stronghold embodies the prevailing military architecture of the time, and includes a moat, a drawbridge, and thick walls that slope toward their mid-section. Added in the 17C, the watch tower (now a bell tower) is crowned by a female-shaped weathervane created in 1632 by sculptor Jerónimo Martínez Pinzón; it is a copy of the **Giraldilla**, symbol of Havana, which was likely modeled on Doña Isabel de Bobadilla *(see sidebar below)*. The original weathervane stands on a plinth inside the entrance to the fort. Devoted to the fort's history as well as shipwrecks and their salvaged goods, the museum features, among other exhibits, a large, lit

First Female Governor

Doña Isabel de Bobadilla was the wife of Hernando de Soto, the Spanish governor who ordered the city to be fortified in 1538. When her husband left for Florida on official business, Dona Isabel took over his duties, thereby becoming the first woman to rule Cuba. Every day she climbed the tall tower of the fortress in hopes of catching sight of the ship bearing her loved one home. The couple exchanged many letters of endearment, some of which reached Doña Isabel long after the death of her husband. De Soto perished far away on the banks of the Mississippi River in 1542.

Castillo de la Real Fuerza

model of the *Santísima Trinidad*, which sank after the Battle of Trafalgar; cases overflowing with gold coins; and excellent illustrations.

From the top of the fort, you can enjoy an expansive view of Old Havana and the forts on the opposite side of the harbor.

Castillo de San Salvador de la Punta

Northern end of the Prado.
Closed temporarily to the public.

Guarding the western side of Havana Bay, at the point *(la punta)* where the bay meets the Straits of Florida, this fortification was erected between 1590 and 1630. It was built as a reinforcement, and is part of the same defense system as the Castillo de los Tres Reyes del Morro on the other side of the bay. Strategically situated to defend the entrance to Havana harbor, both forts were designed by Italian-born Bautista Antonelli, a prominent military engineer in the service of the king of Spain. The smaller of the pair, San Salvador was redesigned as an artillery keep when hurricane damage and construction delays resulted in the scaling back of its original size. The British invasion in 1762 inflicted further harm to the stronghold, which, nevertheless, continued to be used for defense purposes until the 19C. Restored extensively in 2002, the fort retains its four pointed bulwarks, interior plaza, surrounding moat and a series of cannons.

Castillo de San Salvador de la Punta

Castillo de los Tres Reyes del Morro★

Accessible by the Havana bay 🚇 tunnel. Open daily 9am–6pm. 4CUC (lighthouse 2CUC).

A giant chain that blocked the entrance to Havana harbor formerly linked the Castillo de San Salvador de la Punta to this stone fort, which was also designed by Bautista Antonelli. Named for the Magi, or Three Kings *(Tres Reyes)*, in the Bible, El Morro was constructed over 40 years, between 1589 and 1630, atop a steep promontory *(morro)*. Contoured to the shape of the rocky headland on which it perches, the fort is enclosed with thick seawalls. Stepped batteries, a deep moat and a waterside tower (later replaced by a lighthouse) are other features of the stronghold that enabled it to withstand endless attacks by pirates, as well as a lengthy siege by the British in 1762.

A visit to the ramparts includes access to the lighthouse, erected on the point in the mid-19C. From this spot extends an exceptional **view★★** of Havana. **Los Doce Apóstoles** (the Twelve Apostles) restaurant is tucked within the rampart walls; it was named for the 12 cannons mounted here to defend the city. Despite such heavy artillery, Havana fell to British invaders in 1762 when a mine was detonated under a rampart. Its impact is still visible in the ground today. When King Carlos III regained possession of Havana the following year, he ordered construction of La Cabaña, a new fort just south of this site.

Fortaleza de San Carlos de la Cabaña

About a 15min walk southeast of El Morro fort. Open daily 10am –10pm. 4CUC before 6pm, 5CUC after 6pm. Cannon ceremony at 9pm.

Begun in 1763 after the end of British occupation, this massive fortress ranks as the largest in all of Latin America. Designed by Spanish military engineer Don Silvestre Abarca, it measures 700m/2,297ft in length. Named for Spain's King Carlos III, it was never attacked, primarily because,

Castillo de los Tres Reyes del Morro

©Austrophoto/F1 Online/Photononstop

Plucky Pirates, Indeed

Havana was the most important port in the New World in the 16C. Spanish ships, laden with silver and other riches from the Americas, departed Cuba for the courts of Spain, whose kings, through conquest and plunder, had declared dominion over these new-found lands.

Known as the Exterminating Angel, Frenchman **Jacques de Sores**—the most recognized pirate in Cuba—ransacked Havana in 1555, burning temples, plundering icons and robbing chalices from churches. On the morning of July 10, 1555, the watchman at El Morro, at the mouth of the harbor, signaled the arrival of an incoming ship. The Spanish governor fled the Old Fort (the predecessor to La Fuerza), and Sores' mates burned the fortress. After an attempt at a truce failed, Sores set fire to boats in the port. In the devastation, the city archives were lost.

At the behest of Queen Elizabeth I, Englishman Sir Francis Drake, known as the Terror of the Seas, attempted to enter Havana harbor in 1586, but the Cubans were well prepared, and he eventually slipped away.

Welsh privateer Henry Morgan also attacked Cuba, raiding modern-day Camagüey. In 1608 the French pirate Gilberto Girón kidnapped a bishop near Bayamo. Girón demanded a ransom, but the Bayamese rescued the bishop, and a man named Salvador Golomón killed Girón.

The story is the inspiration for Cuba's first written poem *Espejo de Paciencia (Mirror of Patience)* by Silvestre de Balboa.

---

by the time of its completion in 1774, the threat of invasion had greatly subsided. Following the Cuban Revolution, Che Guevara established his headquarters here for several months, and the fort served as a military prison for the new Republic.

About the size of a small village, the complex is lined with cobblestone streets edged by what were once barracks for garrisoned soldiers; there is also a chapel on the grounds. Today cafes, shops and museums occupy the former billeting quarters. The **Museo de la Comandancia del Che Guevara** traces the life of the famed guerilla leader by way of photos, documents and objects from that turbulent period, as well as some of Guevara's personal belongings. Also on the grounds, the **Parque Histórico Militar Morro Cabaña** displays a fine collection of arms that depicts Cuba's military history since colonization. An interesting scale model shows the various stages of Havana's development. Complete with staff in period uniforms, the ceremonial **firing of the cannon** (nightly 9pm) is a custom maintained from the Spanish era when a shot fired from a cannon signaled the closing of the city's gates.

Havana holds an additional fort, the **Castillo del Príncipe** (See Districts, Vedado), which is located southwest of the university in Vedado. Designed by the same engineer as the Fortaleza, the small bastion was begun four years after the Spanish regained the city from the British in 1763. Now in a military zone, it is off-limits to the public.

REVOLUTIONARY SITES

Cuba has witnessed its share of revolts. A pantheon of past heroes who aided the country's independence movements are revered throughout the island today. In Havana, several monuments, memorials, statues and streets are named in their honor. These individuals embody the bravery and determination that has characterized the people of Cuba ever since native chieftain Hatuey organized resistance to Spanish invaders in the early 16C. Public holidays marking their historic actions are occasions to gather in Havana's open forums like the Plaza de la Revolución to celebrate events that changed the course of the country. To all Cubans, the Revolution refers to the success of Fidel Castro and his rebels over government forces, when they triumphantly entered Havana on January 2, 1959. The Revolution is, in fact, referred to by Cubans as the *triunfo de la Revolución*.

Sites in Old Havana

Parque Céspedes
In Plaza de Armas, between Calles O'Reilly and Obispo.
The defined garden within the Plaza de Armas at Old Havana's north end was named in 1923 for sugar-grower **Carlos Manuel de Céspedes**.

On October 10, 1868, Céspedes rang his plantation bell in Cuba's eastern province, not to summon his slaves to work, but to give them their freedom. Céspedes placed himself at the head of a tiny army, determined to liberate his country from the colonial yoke, and in doing so, set in motion the events that became known as the **Ten Years War** (1868-1878). The rebels, poorly equipped, never succeeded in mounting a strong unified offensive and suffered the loss of several of their leaders, including Céspedes, who was shot by the Spanish in 1874.

Erected in 1935, a white marble **statue** in the center of the plaza honors the fallen leader.

▷ *Walk north to Parque de los Mártires.*

Parque de los Mártires
This park at the tip of the Malecón, awkwardly stranded amid road junctions and the entrance to the tunnel under the bay, holds in its center an imposing **statue** of General **Máximo Gómez**, a hero of Cuba's **second war of**

Cuba's First Hero

No visitor to Cuba can fail to notice the defiant-looking native chieftain depicted on the beer bottles from the Hatuey brewery. A *cacique* (chief) who originally came from Santo Domingo, **Hatuey** took the lead in resisting the advance of the Spanish army under the command of Diego Velázquez de Cuellar in 1511. He and his followers sustained a siege of several months in the Baracoa area before retreating into the mountains. Eventually captured, he was burned at the stake. A symbol of Cuban fortitude, he is the first in a long line of heroes who fought for the island's independence.

Museo de la Revolución

independence (1895-1898), who in 1895, together with José Martí and Antonio Maceo, led an army bent on liberating Cuba from east to west.

To the left the **Medical Students' Memorial** was raised to commemorate the young men in the Independence movement who were executed by the Spaniards in 1871.

◯ *Walk south on Avenida de las Misiones and turn right on Calle Refugio.*

Museo de la Revolución★
1 Calle Refugio. Open daily 10am–5pm. 5CUC.
If you visit only one history museum in Havana, this should be your choice. The museum is housed in the former presidential palace, the splendid 1913 **Palacio Presidencial**★, designed by Cuban Rodolfo Maruri and Paul Belau of Belgium. The interior was done by Tiffany's of New York. Cuba's presidents resided here from 1920 to 1965. In 1957 the

building witnessed a failed assassination attempt by the rebels on the life of Cuban dictator **Fulgencio Batista** during his second term as president (1952-1959).

All four stories are devoted to the museum's chronology of Cuba's history, from the colonial period through to the Revolution.

Interior, Museo de la Revolución

REVOLUTIONARY SITES

79

Photographs, historical objects and documents are on view as well as a diorama of **Che Guevara** and **Camilo Cienfuegos** emerging from the forest of the Sierra Maestra.

A corridor leads to the **Granma Memorial**. It passes en route the Rincón de los Cretinos (cretins corner), where unflattering caricatures of Batista and former US presidents Ronald Reagan and George Bush pay sarcastic homage to leaders whose policies fomented the Cuban Revolution or ran contrary to the political stance of Cuba's current regime.

Outside, beneath a glass pavilion, you'll find the *Granma*, the 20m/65ft **yacht** that carried Fidel Castro and 81 fellow revolutionaries from Mexico to Playa Las Coloradas (Granma province) in 1956 in an ill-fated attempt to start an uprising. Displayed around the memorial are various means of transportation and weaponry that were used in revolutionary conflicts, including a truck involved in the attack on the presidential palace in 1957 and an airplane used during the attack on the Bay of Pigs.

Sites in Vedado

Plaza de la Revolución

This immense, 4.5ha/11acre esplanade has accommodated nearly a million attendees at political demonstrations and cultural events. Teeming throngs of Cubans flock here on annual commemorative events held January 1, May 1 and July 26 *(see Calendar of Events)*.

At other times, visitors come to stop and admire the José Martí Memorial or the iron sculpture portraits of Che Guevara and Camilo Cienfuegos, the third of the trio of *los barbudos* (the bearded), as Fidel, Che and Camilo were known. Construction began on the Plaza de la Revolución in the 1950s during the Batista regime, but wasn't completed until after Fidel Castro came to power.

At the southern edge, a gigantic marble **statue** marks the **Memorial de José Martí** *(open Mon–Sat 9:30am–5pm; 3CUC)*, the memorial itself a huge, five-sided obelisk 109m/358ft tall. Martí was a key figure in the renewed struggle for independence after the formal ending of the Ten Years

Plaza de la Revolución

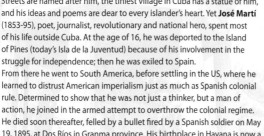

The Apostle of Independence

Streets are named after him, the tiniest village in Cuba has a statue of him, and his ideas and poems are dear to every islander's heart. Yet **José Martí** (1853-95), poet, journalist, revolutionary and national hero, spent most of his life outside Cuba. At the age of 16, he was deported to the Island of Pines (today's Isla de la Juventud) because of his involvement in the struggle for independence; then he was exiled to Spain.

From there he went to South America, before settling in the US, where he learned to distrust American imperialism just as much as Spanish colonial rule. Determined to show that he was not just a thinker, but a man of action, he joined in the armed attempt to overthrow the colonial regime. He died soon thereafter, felled by a bullet fired by a Spanish soldier on May 19, 1895, at Dos Ríos in Granma province. His birthplace in Havana is now a small museum *(see Museums)*.

War. Spending most of his life in exile, he was the driving force behind the Cuban Revolutionary Party, which he founded in 1892. (Another statue of Martí stands in the middle of Parque Central: *see Parksand Gardens*.)

The **museum** within celebrates the life of this "apostle of independence," with personal artifacts and photographs that supplement videos and recordings. From the top of the memorial (*2CUC*), the view extends over the concrete government buildings that surround the plaza, as well as all of Havana.

On the north side of the plaza, the façade of the Ministry of the Interior bears the **portrait of Che Guevara,** an immense sculpture in black metal.

The exterior of the adjacent Ministry of Communications building now displays a black metal **portrait of Camilo Cienfuegos,** who died in a mysterious plane crash off the coast of Cuba on October 28, 1959. No wreckage or remains were ever found.

Palacio de la Revolución

To the south of the Plaza de la Revolución sits this vast building, which serves as the seat of the Central Committee of the Cuban Communist Party and the offices of the president.

©Sylvaine Poitau/Apa Publications

Memorial de José Martí, Plaza de la Revolución

MUSEUMS

Most visitors don't come to Havana to spend all day indoors. It's the lively streets and promenades, the craft and vegetable markets and the crowded plazas that reveal the character and lives of habaneros. But you would be remiss if you didn't at least sample the city's artistic and historical treasures that have been preserved for posterity. After you visit the Museo de la Revolución *(see Revolutionary Sites)*, a definite Must See, take time to explore at least one or two of the museums described below. You'll have a better appreciation of the cultural riches of the Cuban people and their past. Yet, be advised that viewing the splendid collections of the Museo Nacional de Bellas Artes, exhibited in two locations, could easily fill most of the day.

Art Museums

The following museums are dedicated to showcasing Cuban arts and international works.

Museo Nacional de Bellas Artes★★ (Arte Universal)
Calle San Rafael between Calle Zulueta and Monserrate, La Habana Vieja. Open Tue–Sat 10am–6pm, Sun 10am–2pm. 5CUC, or 8CUC combined ticket for both locations. (7) 861 0241.
Cuba's National Museum of Fine Arts has amassed nearly 50,000 works of art. Not only are the

substantial holdings of Havana's principal art museum divided into two categories—international (Arte Universal) and Cuban (Arte Cubano)—they are also housed in two separate buildings that sit a couple of blocks apart.
The international collections are installed in the former **Centro Asturiano** (1927), which faces the Edificio Manzana de Gómez opposite Parque Central. Occupying a full block, the stately building was designed by Spanish architect Manuel del Busto. The exterior exhibits Classical features

Museo Nacional de Bellas Artes (Arte Universal)

Allow 4 hours to visit the **Museo Nacional de Bellas Artes**. You might want to see the international collections first, and then walk the two blocks to the Cuban collections. There you can have lunch in the on-site cafeteria before viewing the Cuban art. The works in the museum are labeled only in Spanish. Guidebooks *(in Spanish)* to the collections can be purchased in the museum shop at each location. You can hire an English-speaking guide to take you through the highlights of the collection (best if arranged in advance of your visit).

of the Spanish Renaissance style, but is embellished with Baroque ornamentation, especially on its towers. The building was built for a social club for wealthy Spaniards similar to the Galicians club *(see Gran Teatro)* and evidences the expense patrons lavished on the structure's exterior and interior. Indeed, the museum's handsome interior spaces are perfect for wandering and perusing the varied and exquisite works of art.

The vast entry hall features an imposing staircase and, above it, a magnificent **stained-glass window**★★ illustrating the arrival of Christopher Columbus. Exhibited over five floors, the works are divided by the artist's native country. On the ground floor, you can explore the interesting collection of **South American religious art.** Contemporary art exhibition galleries are also located on the ground floor and in the library. On the second floor, displayed in airy, modern galleries, **objects of Antiquity**★★ include Greek statues, Roman mosaics, Coptic tapestries, talismans and Egyptian funerary vases as well as Sumerian tablets.

The mezzanine presents works from the various schools of **German painting,** including a fine 16C **crucifixion**★★ by Lucas Cranach the Elder. An important collection of 18C **English paintings**★ includes portraits by Reynolds and Gainsborough. Among the **Italian paintings**★★ is Canaletto's *Chelsea from the Thames* (1751). **French painting**★★ is also represented; notable works include *Vue du Pont de Nantes* by Corot (1855) and *La Vague* by Courbet (1854).

The **Spanish painting**★★ galleries feature splendid pieces by Ribera (17C), Zurbarán (17C) and Sorolla (19C).

Museo Nacional de Bellas Artes★★ (Arte Cubano)
Avenida de las Misiones and Trocadero, La Habana Vieja. Open Tues–Sat 10am–6pm, Sun 10am–2pm. 5CUC, 8CUC combined ticket with international collections.
The national art museum's Cuban collections are housed in a large, gray, modern structure dating from the 1950s. Inside, airy galleries on three floors display extensive selections of Cuban art from the 16C to the present. Be sure to see the works by Wifredo Lam in particular.

On the third floor, one gallery is devoted to paintings from the colonial period (16C-19C), mostly of religious scenes or portraits of

MUSEUMS

Museo de Bellas Artes (Arte Cubano)

the aristocracy. Another showcases turn-of-the-19C works by artists such as Armando García Menocal and Leopoldo Romañach. Modern works are represented by such artists as Amelia Peláez, René Portocarrero, Zaida del Río and Victor Manuel García (who painted the iconic *Gitana Tropical* in 1929). The museum is especially rich in art of the 20C with pieces by Wifredo Lam (1902-82). The contemporary art gallery includes works by Esterio Segura, José Manuel Fors Durán and Tania Brugera.

Museo de Artes Decorativas★★
Calle 17 between D and E, Vedado. Open Tue–Sat 10am–5pm. 3CUC.
The rooms in this sumptuous former residence dating from the 1920s were created by Paris' famed Maison Jansen interior decorating firm in the 20C. The fine 18C furnishings are the work of celebrated French cabinetmakers such as Boudin, Chevalier and

Simoneau. You'll also find exquisite gold-plated pieces and porcelains by Sèvres. The home's elegant décor and objets d'art provide a snapshot of high society life in Havana in pre-Revolutionary days, as it was the home of Countess María Luisa Gómez-Mena, a sister of the sugar baron José Gómez-Mena Vila. The upstairs bathroom is constructed entirely of marble, including the tub. Behind the mansion, the gardens hint at their former grandeur.

Museo de la Cerámica Contemporánea Cubana★
Calle Mercaderes and Calle Amargura, La Habana Vieja. Open Tue–Sat 9am–5pm, Sun 9am–1pm.
Housed in the Casa Aguilera, a beautiful Spanish Colonial mansion on a corner lot, the Ceramics Museum presents a collection of works by Cuban artists, mostly of the 20C, such as Wifredo Lam and Amelia

Peláez. In addition to traditional works, many of the pieces have a dreamlike or sensual quality to them. Notable works include *El Pan Nuestro* (1991) by Angel R. Oliva depicting a disintegrating helmet surrounded by a knife and fork on a table mat of tiny conjoined skulls. Rafael Miranada's *Sentimientos Ocultos* (2001) illustrates a statue of an artist's head atop a torso of a woman with a man's calves and feet; her womb is cut open to reveal a real human fetus inside a box, viewed through glass at head height. The rooms downstairs host temporary exhibits.

Museo de la Danza
Avenida de los Presidentes and Calle Linea, Vedado. Open Tue–Sat 10am–6pm. 2CUC.
Founded in conjuction with the 50th anniversary of the National Ballet of Cuba, this museum pays tribute to **Alicia Alonso** (b.1920), famed ballet diva and longtime director of the national ballet. Photographs, artifacts, costumes and paintings depict the history of Cuban and international ballet. The stage set drawings are the highlight, including one in ink and tempera by Salvador Fernandez for *Giselle*. The Alicia Alonso salon displays a glittering array of headpieces, medals and other memorabilia, including a photograph of Alonso's last public dance in Italy in 1995. There is also a collection of black and white images of 28 of Cuba's prima ballerinas.

Museo Nacional de la Música
Corner of Avenidas de las Misiones and de Cárcel, La Habana Vieja. Under long-term renovation.

The Italian Renaissance-style façade of this small, elegant house (1905), which is named **Casa de Pérez de la Riva★**, strikes an anachronistic note within the surrounding, heavily trafficked thoroughfares. The casa is home to Cuba's national museum of music, whose eclectic collections include pianos, Indian sitars, Haitian tambours, balalaikas and other Cuban and foreign musical instruments as well as music boxes, musical scores and photos of musicians. Concerts are held in a temporary venue at 509 Calle Obrapia, between Calles Bernaza and Villegas, where programs are posted in the window.

Museums to Men
The following museums pay tribute to larger-than-life men whose accomplishments were intertwined with Cuba at some point in time.

Museo José Martí - Casa Natal de José Martí★
314 Calle Leonor Pérez, La Habana Vieja. Open Tue–Sat 9:30am–5pm, Sun 9:30am–12:45pm. 1CUC. (7) 861 5095.
On January 28, 1853, the "apostle of Cuban Independence" was born in this small house and spent the first four years of his life here. The museum, established in 1925, preserves several of his personal belongings that are intimately linked with the history of the island. Among the photographs, note that there is just one of Martí smiling, with his son upon his knee. Also housed here is the only known portrait of Martí, painted by the Swedish artist Hermann Norman in 1891.

MUSEUMS

Havana's Art Scene

The creative scene in Havana is thriving. Finding your way around the best exhibits of the city's avant-garde artists is difficult though. Curator **Sussette Martínez** *(7 267 7989, www.art-havana.com)* takes visitors to studios of working artists with a view toward learning about their individual art and buying Cuban art.

The following galleries showcase mainly rotating exhibits:

Galería La Acacia (Map II, A3), *114 Calle San José, between Calles Industria and Consulado. Mon–Fri and every other Sat 10am–4pm.* Sale of art plus works by major Cuban artists. High prices.

Galería La Casona (Map II, C3), *107 Calles Muralla and San Ignacio, (7) 862 2633. Tue–Sat 9am–5pm. May be closed for repairs.* This 18C palace houses four galleries: the most interesting one (contemporary art) is upstairs, over the patio.

Galería Habana (Map IV, A1), *460 Calle Línea, between Calles E and F, (7) 832 7101, www. galeriahabana.com. Mon–Sat 10am–4:30pm, Sun 9am–1pm.* The gallery receives the cream of the crop in contemporary Cuban art: Los Carpinteros, Choco, Carlos Quintana, etc.

Centro de Arte Contemporáneo Wifredo Lam *(Map III, A1), Calles San Ignacio and Empedrado.* Contemporary art.

Casa de Guayasamín (Map III, B2), *Calle Obrapía, between Mercaderes and Oficios.* Ecuadorian Oswaldo Guayasamin (1919-99) is famous for his portrait of Fidel; portraits of Fidel and Raúl Castro are upstairs.

Factoria Habana, *Calle O'Reilly 308, between Habana and Aguiar, La Habana Vieja, (7) 8649518, www.factoriahabana.ohc.cu. Mon–Sat 9:30am–5pm.* This new space in a converted paper factory exhibits contemporary art in the form of installations and sculptures.

Galería 23 and 12, *Calle 23 at the corner of Calle 12, Vedado. (7) 831 1810.* Consult www.opushabana.cu, www.cubanow.net, and www.cubabsolutely.com for other listings.

Museo Napoleónico★

1159 Calle San Miguel, at corner of Ronda, Vedado. Open Tue–Sat 9:30am–5pm, Sun 9:30am–12:30pm. 3CUC (7) 879 1460. Behind the University of Havana campus rises a Florentine-style palace, recently and superbly restored. It houses one of the world's most extensive collections of Napoleon Bonaparte memorabilia and artifacts. The collection was amassed by Cuban Julio Lobo, a wealthy sugar tycoon and aficionado of all things Napoleon whose fortune allowed

Interior, Museo Napoleónico

©Claire Boobbyer/Michelin

him to purchase curios, antiques and busts on trips abroad. Built in 1928, the Italianate mansion belonged to Orestes Ferrara, who acquired Lobo's collection. Ferrara was a Neapolitan who fought for the Cubans in the 1898 Spanish American War.

The museum's salons are filled with Empire-style furnishings and Sèvres porcelains. Browse among the drawings and tapestries on the third floor to find the painting by Jean-Georges Vibert depicting the emperor preparing for his coronation. The museum also displays one of Bonaparte's bronze death masks; the sight of it surprises many visitors, positioned as it is on a table next to Napoleon's bed.

According to John Paul Rathbone's fascinating book about Lobo, *The Sugar King of Havana,* Bonaparte's last doctor, Corsican Francesco Antommarchi, retired to Cuba, bringing the death mask with him. The library houses numerous volumes on the life and times of Napoleon.

Museo Hemingway★

Calles Vigía and Steimbert, in San Francisco de Paula, 🔾 *13km/ 8mi southeast of Havana* (see North Coast Map). *From the road to Guanabacoa, exit via Blanca, about half a mile (800m) after the Luyano River. Take the Central Road to the right, in the direction of Parque Virgen del Camino and continue straight ahead, following the signs for Guines. Open Mon– Sat 10am–5pm, Sun 10am–1pm. Guided tour 3CUC. (7) 691 0809. Do not visit if it is raining: shutters will be closed.*

> **The Old Man and the Sea**
> The skipper of Ernest Hemingway's yacht, the *Pilar,* for nearly 30 years, **Gregorio Fuentes** accompanied Hemingway on all his outings at sea. Only after the writer's death did he cease piloting the boat. The fisherman served as the model for the main character of Hemingway's famous novel *The Old Man and the Sea,* which earned the author the Nobel Prize for Literature in 1954. Fuentes died in 2002, his face furrowed by years of sun and spray, at the age of 104.

In 1939 American author Ernest Hemingway moved to the Finca la Vigía, a hilltop property. After his return to the US in 1960, the house was transformed into a museum commemorating his years in Cuba. Furnishings, personal artifacts and memorabilia remain as they were when Hemingway lived here. Visitors may not enter the house, but can peer through the **open windows** from outside.

Among the laden bookshelves and hunting trophies, look for Hemingway's typewriter and his beloved guns. The author set up an office in the tower behind the house.

Also on the property, which is lushly planted with palms, you'll see his small yacht, the *Pilar,* and the gravesites of his four dogs.

MUSEUMS

LANDMARKS WITH A BEAT

Havana is a city entwined in music and dance. Every habanero seems born with an innate sense of rhythm, which finds ready expression in the city's many street and professional musicians and dancers. The modern world has grown up with the sounds of Afro-Cuban music—from salsa and son to rumba and Latin jazz. It would be unfortunate if visitors did not rediscover something of themselves in the beats throbbing throughout the city's streets, bars and casas de la música. Here are some places to make those rediscoveries— venues that have stood the test of time *(see also Nightlife)*.

The High Notes

Premier clubs can usually attract the most in-demand musicians, which in turn causes the cover charge to be higher than other venues. *For tips about cover charges, dress code, etc., see p125.*

Café Cantante
Paseo and Avenida 39, Vedado. (7) 878 4275. http://promociones. egrem.co.cu. 5-10CUC.
The biggest salsa groups play in this basement hall beneath the Teatro Nacional in the Plaza de la Revolución. The lively nightspot hosts live bands most nights. Its matinee performances are always crowded with Cubans. Proper dress is required: no shorts or T-shirts.

Casa de la Música Habana
Calle Galiano, between Calles Concordia and Neptuno, Centro Habana. (7) 860 8296. http://promociones.egrem.co.cu. 5-20CUC, depending upon the band.
Run by the state recording company EGREM, this very popular spot often hosts bands that are the latest rage, and it has a large dance floor as well. As a consequence, long lines of people wait to get in. The weekly program is posted on the door, and there's a shop selling CDs and instruments next door. There is a second location in Miramar at **Avenida 35** *(7 204 0447)*, but the Centro venue sees more locals.

Casa de la Música Habana

© Christian Heeb/hemis.fr

Buena Vista Social Club

In 1997, American guitarist Ry Cooder and Cuban musician Juan de Marcos González came up with an album entitled *Buena Vista Social Club*. It featured recordings of veteran musicians and singers Ibrahim Ferrer, Compay Segundo, Omara Portuondo, Rubén González and Eliades Ochoa, who had been famous in the 1930s through the 1950s, during Cuba's golden age of music. Their performance was captured on film by German director Wim Wenders in 1999. The huge success of both the album (7 million copies sold) and the film (Academy Award nomination for Best Documentary feature), which included moving interviews of the aging artists, sparked a revival of international interest in traditional Cuban music.

Hotel Nacional★
Calle 21 and Calle O, Vedado. (7) 836 3564. www.hotelnacional decuba.com.
Every Thursday and Saturday evening (9pm), the hotel presents live Cuban music in its **Salón 1930** or **Compay Segundo Hall**. Usually featured is an orchestra or band, such as musicians from the renowned Buena Vista Social Club, as well as dancers and a singer. Look for flyers at the tour desks in all the hotels surrounding Parque Central.

Dance the Night Away
Here are a few Havana venues whose dance floors can get crowded and quite boisterous.

Casa de la Amistad
406 Avenida Paseo, between Calle 17 and Calle 19, Vedado. 3-10CUC
Most nights, Cubans pack the grounds of this stately mansion, designed in the 1920s in the Italianate style; the interior, however, is an Art Deco gem, with a beautiful **staircase** that curves elegantly to the first floor.
The former residence of landowner Juan Pedro Baró was converted by the government into an outdoor performance venue that is now a popular place to listen and dance to traditional music (rumba, son and salsa) played by excellent bands. Have a drink in the lovely garden before stepping onto the dance floor.

Callejón de Hamel★
On Hamel, between Calles Aramburu and Hospital, near Calle San Lázaro, Centro Habana.
Against a backdrop of Salvador González Escalona's colorful murals *(see Districts, Centro Habana)*, crowds gather every Sunday at noon for live rumba performances in this small alley in Centro Habana. The street soon is hopping with spontaneous dancing among the audience. It's best to get here *before* noon on Sunday, though, if you want a good view of the action, and be sure to bring a hat (there is no shade).
The nearby **El Negrón bar** serves a cocktail called *negrón* made of lemon, honey, basil and rum.

Sábado de la Rumba
El Gran Palenque, Calle 4, between Calles Calzada and Avenida 5, Vedado (7) 863 5953. 5CUC.
Arrayed in colorful costumes,

What Makes Afro-Cuban Music?

The sound of drums dominates Afro-Cuban music. Shaped like a tall barrel and held between the legs, the **conga** *(tumbadora)* lays down the basic rhythm. Consisting of two small round drums of unequal size and linked together, the **bongo** is supported on the drummer's knees.

The **timbales** are a pair of side drums mounted on a stand. Batons of hardened wood, the **claves** are tapped against each other to make a five-note beat—the sharp metallic sound that lays down the basic rhythm of son and salsa. The **güiro** is a ribbed and elongated, hollowed-out gourd that is scraped with a stick, and the **maracas,** filled with seeds, are used like a rattle. The trumpet, saxophone, piano, double-bass, violin and flute all play their part in Cuban music, as does the **tres,** a small guitar with three sets of double strings.

members of the celebrated ensemble **Conjunto Folklorico Nacional de Cuba** *(see Performing Arts)* dance the rumba in electrifying fashion here every Saturday (3pm). They are sometimes joined by soloists and other performers. Come early for a seat, or it's standing room only at this popular weekly show. You may be inspired to take lessons from the group, not only in rumba, but also mambo, cha-cha-chá, and other Latin dances. For a schedule, www.folkcuba.cult.cu (in English).

Asociación Cultura Yoruba de Cuba
615 Prado, between Calles Monte and Dragones, Centro Habana. (7) 863 5953. www.cubayoruba.cult.cu.
Folkloric dancing takes place here Thursdays and Sundays between 5pm and 8pm. *Tambores* are ceremonies that honor the *orishas (see sidebar p94)* using the ritual drums of Santería, the *batáa*. The *fiestas de santo* honor individual *orishas,* and take place at 4pm on the day divined for the celebration.

Though you may not actually dance, the music is so infectious you may find yourself at least swaying to it.

Easy Listening
These venues are primarily for jazz lovers.

Delirio Habanero
3rd floor, Teatro National, corner of Paseo and Avenida 39, Vedado. (7) 878 4275. 5-15CUC.
This low-lit piano bar on the third floor of the Teatro Nacional appeals to a sophisticated crowd seeking a relaxing, low-key evening of music. Jazz is the primary offering here, either from the piano or a live quartet. *Reservations essential on weekends.*

La Zorra y el Cuervo
Corner of Calle 23 and Calle O, Vedado. (7) 833 2402. 10pm–1am. 10CUC (includes a drink).
Jazz and nothing but jazz is performed here on weekends, with Afro-Cuban rhythms filling the gaps between sets. Jazz aficionados in the know make their way here to hear the seductive

vocalists of the Sexto Sentido quartet, or the extraordinary piano mastery of Roberto Fonseca, who accompanied renowned Buena Vista Social Club singer Ibrahim Ferrer on his final recording.

Come to the Cabaret

Cabaret Parisien
Hotel Nacional, Calle 21 and Calle O, Vedado (7) 836 3663. www.hotelnacionaldecuba.com. 35CUC (with meal 55CUC).
Nightly the hotel presents Cabaret Parisien, a two-hour extravaganza entitled "Cuban, Cubano" starting at 10pm. At the show's end at midnight, you can take dancing lessons. Every Sunday at 7pm, jazz musicians from the cabaret program perform in the hotel garden.

Tropicana
Corner of Calle 72 and Avenida 43, Marianao. (7) 267 1010. www.cabaret-tropicana.com. 50-60CUC (with meal from 70CUC)
Opened in 1939, the world-famous Tropicana has been a showcase for international stars like Nat King Cole, Josephine Baker, Liberace and Maurice Chevalier.
Nowadays it puts on the most spectacular feathers and sequins show in Cuba, featuring more than 200 elaborately costumed (but skimpily dressed) dancers in an open-air setting of tropical greenery.
Even though the venue is located some distance from Havana proper and admission is expensive, the shows are often fully booked, so reserve well in advance.

Traditional Tunes

Café Taberna
531 Calle Mercaderes, Teniente Rey (Brasil), La Habana Vieja. (7) 861 1637.
An institution, this restaurant has been in business on La Plaza Vieja since 1777. It is known for its house bands specializing in son. Twice a day these musicians, devoted fans of Cuban great Benny Moré, entertain diners with his music and other traditional Cuban tunes. The sounds can get quite loud, so you may want to ask for a table at the rear.

El Jelengue de Areito
410 Calle San Miguel, between Calles Campanario and Lealtad, Centro Habana. (7) 862 0673. 20CUP.
This new Egrem-run space treats music lovers to the sounds of son, trova, **bolero**, salsa, rumba and more in the small covered yard, the back wall of which is lined with album covers. There's live music from 5pm to 7pm, and the Friday matinee rumba is especially popular.

© Ellen Rooney/AGE Fotostock

Tropicana show

PARKS AND GARDENS

The typical Spanish colonial town in Cuba was laid out on a grid pattern with streets intersecting at right angles. At its heart was a *parque central,* a spacious square usually with a formal garden in the middle. Havana was no exception, and in addition to its Parque Central, the capital area maintains several large urban parks that offer shade, beauty and recreation as well as opportunities for strolling, socializing and people-watching. Well to the south of the city proper, the country's botanical garden is worth a visit, especially if you are interested in Cuba's flora.

Havana Havens

Parque Central★
Bounded by Calles Obrapía, Agramonte, Neptuno and the Prado.

Occupying two equally divided city blocks diagonally opposite the Capitolio's northeast side, this formal park-plaza is truly a focal point, straddling both Old Havana and Centro Habana along the busy Prado. Lined with stately Royal palm trees *(see sidebar below)* and wrought-iron street lamps, its center focuses on the **statue of José Martí,** erected in 1905 to honor the Cuban hero of the independence movement. Several monumental buildings face the park: the **Gran Teatro** *(see Cuban ClassicS)* in the southwest corner; north of it, **Hotel Inglaterra** (1875), Havana's oldest hotel *(see Hotels)* and the restored blue Hotel Telégrafo; its northern reach faces the large, modern mustard-yellow Hotel Parque Central that occupies an entire block. Its northeast corner is dominated by the angular Hotel Plaza *(See Hotels),* also one of the city's oldest hotels. Opposite the Hotel Plaza, on the northwest edge of the park, is the Edificio Manzana de Gómez, a large run-down shopping arcade; and south

Parque Central

©Claire Boobbyer/Michelin

of it, the **Museo Nacional de Bellas Artes** *(see Museums)*. Cubans populate the park at all hours of the day and night, enjoying the peace and quiet and an opportunity to mingle with their friends. On the south side, by a long line of benches, the *esquina caliente* (literally "hot corner") is full of Cuban men shouting at each other, not in anger, but in heated debate about the latest baseball results. Tourists rarely tarry long in Parque Central, though, despite the pleasant shade provided by the bushy gardens at either end of the park. The youthful Habaneros who frequent the public space have the habit of pestering tourists for money or a beer, or asking them to send a letter to a friend in another country.

Parque de la Fraternidad
Between Calle Máximo Gómez (Monte) and Dragones, and bordered by Amistad and Prado.
Situated immediately south of the Capitolio National, this large landscaped park, crisscrossed by roads and taxi parking, is shaded by palm trees. It lies at the south end of the Prado, serving as a central point between Old Havana and Centro Habana. As at the nearby Parque Central, Cubans come here to catch a *botero* (taxi), or just to sit and visit beneath the shade of the palm trees.

In the 18C the site was a military square where soldiers drilled. Named Parque de la Fraternidad (Fraternity Park) in 1928, the park was the realization of Jean-Claude Nicolas Forestier's *(see sidebar)* design, and included statuary of Venezuelan Simón Bolívar, American Abraham Lincoln and other symbols of freedom on the grounds.

At the park's center stands a magnificent **ceiba tree** planted on February 24, 1928, during the sixth Pan-American Conference. On a traffic island at the southeast corner facing the Hotel Saratoga, a marble fountain named the **Fuente de la India** was created by Italian sculptor Giuseppe Gaggini in 1837. Known as Noble Havana, the figure of a native woman holds a shield bearing Havana's coat of arms, and is considered the symbol of the city. Next to the Hotel Saratoga, and opposite the park, sits the **Asociación Cultura Yoruba de Cuba** *(open daily 9am–5pm; 10CUC).*

93

Situated in the middle of Parque Lenin, **Las Ruinas** restaurant *(Calle 100 and Cortina de la Presa; open Tue–Sun noon–3:30pm; 7 644 2721)* occupies a modern building that incorporates the ruins of a former sugar mill. A stained-glass window by Cuban artist René Portocarrero illuminates the dining room. Furnishings from the colonial period and tropical plants lend a certain cachet. The quality of a meal *(30-50CUP)* can be haphazard, but you can always content yourself with a drink on the terrace overlooking the park. *Food must be paid for in Cuban pesos, drinks in CUC.*

As much a cultural center as a museum, the building houses the pantheon of gods *(orishas)* of the Yoruba religion, personified by mannequins in tableaux on the second floor. Other areas include exhibit rooms, craft studios and a library. Every Thursday and Sunday

Parque de la Fraternidad

©Claire Boobbyer/Michelin

afternoon, dance performances are open to the public *(see Landmarks)*. South of the park, at Avenida Simón Bolívar and Calle Amistad, the historic **Palacio de Aldama★★** (Map IV, C2) was erected for Don Domingo de Aldama y Aréchaga. The Neoclassical palace buildings were completed in 1840, but were mobbed in 1869 by the Spanish Volunteers because of Aldama's support for the movement toward Cuban independence. Today it houses the Institute of the History of the Cuban Workers' Movement and of the Socialist Revolution. It is not open to the public.

South Parks

Parque Lenin
Map I, C4. ◗ *25km/15mi south of downtown Havana.*
Follow Avenida Rancho Boyeros (Avenida Independencia) toward the airport. Just past the bridge over the Almendares River, turn left on Avenida San Francisco (Calle 100). Attractions Wed–Sun 10am–5pm.
Located far south of Havana proper, this vast, wooded recreational park was established in 1972. The bust of the park's namesake, Russian revolutionary **Vladimir Lenin** (1870-1924), was carved in 1984 by Lev Kerbel, a sculptor from the then Soviet Union. There is also a small landscaped memorial park built in homage to **Celia Sánchez,** Fidel Castro's secretary during the 1956-59 rebel campaign. Approached by enormous descending stepping stones, a statue of the female revolutionary is embedded in a garden wall covered with plants and ferns.

The 700ha/1,730 acre park was designed with riding stables, swimming pools, an amphitheater, an art gallery, a theater, cafeterias and a restaurant *(see Touring Tip)*, all scattered around an artificial lake. The northern part of the park has a Ferris wheel and other amusement rides for children. When the attractions are not in operation, the park is even emptier and more peaceful than usual. The park's popularity has declined in recent years due to the lack of transportation and the distance from downtown; many of the attractions may be closed.

Parque Lenin
©Claire Boobbyer/Michelin

Jardín Botánico Nacional de Cuba

◗ *3km/2mi southeast of Parque Lenin. Main entrance off Carretera del Rocío. Open daily for tourists 8:30am–4pm. (7) 697 9364. 1CUC. Map of the garden at www.uh.cu/centros/jbn (in Spanish). It's best to see the garden by car or by the park's narrow-gauge train (additional 3CUC). English-speaking guides available. Restaurants and snack bars are open throughout the garden.*

At this 600ha/1,483 acre garden, a great variety of tropical plant specimens from Cuba and around the world are on display. Highlights of the collections include a large number of 🌿 **palm trees, cactus** and succulent plants in greenhouses, plants native to Cuba and the Caribbean, and the remarkable **Japanese Garden.** A gift from the Japanese government in 1989, the garden incorporates traditional Asian elements such as pavilions, rocks and water features. Also on the grounds are an herbarium and a lily pond.

The National Tree

It's difficult to imagine Cuba without its palm trees. Featured on the country's coat of arms, the **Royal palm** *(Roystonea regia)* has become a symbol of the dignity and determination of the Cuban people. With its slender, pale gray trunk and great plume of radiating foliage, it is part of every Cuban landscape. It normally grows up to 25m/82ft high, but often reaches 40m/131ft in height. Perfect rows of majestic Royal palms lining miles of sugar-cane fields is a classic sight, ubiquitous in Cuba. Seventy million palms grow in Cuba, more per square mile than anywhere else on earth. About 100 other species of palm have been recorded on the island, 70 of them endemic.

PARKS AND GARDENS

BEST BEACHES

Just east of Havana, a series of beautiful white-sand beaches extends one after another, making up a famous chain known as the **Playas del Este** (Eastern Beaches). While quieter during the week, the beaches attract crowds of city dwellers on weekends who travel by any means possible—vintage American cars, mopeds, buses and bicycles—to spend time by the sea.. Find your mode of transportation to get here and enjoy a day trip or several days of escape from Havana city life.

🏖 PLAYAS DEL ESTE★

Leave Havana by the harbor tunnel toward the fortresses, and follow the signposts along the Vía Monumental that lead to the **Vía Blanca**. *After 6km/4mi, you'll cross the Bacuranao River, where the first of the beaches are located, only 18km/11mi from the capital. At the mouth of the Bacuranao River, a little cove signals Playa Bacuranao. The Vía Blanca continues inland, parallel to the coast, providing access to all the Atlantic coast beaches.*

The beaches closest to Havana are Cojímar, **Playa Bacuranao**, Playa Tarará, **Playa Santa María del Mar★★** and **Guanabo★** *(see map below)*. The beach at **Jibacoa**, farther east, is more secluded, and is popular for snorkeling. Santa María del Mar is the most attractive of the beaches; most hotels for international visitors are located here *(see Hotels, Playas del Este)*. Hotels in Guanabo welcome Cubans and foreigners, but you'll find several homes with rooms for rent *(casas particulares)* for travelers who want to share the beach with just locals.

Once you've arrived in a beach town, it's easy to get around on foot, but if you want to go from town to town, you'll need a car, taxi, moped, a ride on the **HabanaBusTour** or other means of transport *(see opposite)*.

Playas del Este

©Darius Koehli/AGE Fotostock

MUST SEE

Practical Information

Getting There

◆ **By Car** – The best way to travel the 18km/11mi to 40km/25mi between Havana and the Playas del Este is by car. *See directions opposite.* Hiring a taxi *(see below)* is an alternative.

◆ **By Bus** – HabanaBusTour tourist buses (Line 3), run by **Transtur**, link Havana and the beaches at Cojímar, Bacuranao, and Santa María del Mar *(daily 9am–7pm; 3CUC, ticket valid all day)*. Bus 400 links Havana and Guanabo. The bus stop is located at the corner of Egido and Calle Gloria near the train station. Be prepared to wait.

◆ **By Taxi** – A private taxi *(taxi particular)* is a better choice than an official state taxi for a trip to the beach. If you're going for the day, plan to pay 30CUC–40CUC for a round-trip fare.

Getting Around

◆ **By Taxi** – Cubataxi stands are located in front of most hotels in Santa María del Mar. Cubataxi in Guanabo (7 796 3939).

◆ **By Car** – Transtur rental desks are located in major hotels.

◆ **By Bike** – For rentals, inquire at the Hotel Club Atlántico and at Breezes Jibacoa.

Visitor Information

◆ **Tourist Information** – The major hotels maintain tourist desks where you'll find information on activities, facilities and organized excursions to Havana and other areas. There are Infotur offices in Guanabo and Santa María del Mar.

◆ **Banks/Currency Exchange** – Some hotels offer currency exchange. **Banco de Crédito y Comercio** (D1), Ave. 5ta, between 470 and 472, Guanabo. Cadecas exist at Avenida 5 between Calles 476 and 478 in Guanabo and in Santa María next to the Infotur office. The Guanabo Cadeca has an ATM.

◆ **Health** – Clínica Internacional (A1), 36 Ave. de las Terrazas, Santa María del Mar, *(7) 961 819 ext 102.* Medical services are available in some hotels.

◆ **Servicupet service stations** – **Bacuranao,** Km 15.5 Vía Blanca, Bacuranao. **Gran Via**, Guanabo Rotonda, at the entrance to Guanabo on the road from Havana.

◆ **Accommodations** – Most hotels for international visitors are located in Santa María del Mar. Rates include breakfast. Hotels in Guanabo are spartan, but you'll find several *casas particulares* here. *For a selection of lodgings, see Playas del Este under Hotels.*

◆ **Where to Eat** – Most hotels have restaurants; beachside shacks also provide the makings of a quick meal. You'll find a couple of good *paladares* in Guanabo. *For a selection of restaurants, see Playas del Este under Restaurants.*

Recreation

◆ **Water Sports** – Most hotels offer opportunities for marine sports. In high season there are **Marlin Punto Náutico kiosks** on the beach renting equipment. For scuba diving, snorkeling, fishing and sea excursions, inquire at the **Super-Club Breezes Jibacoa** resort *(see Hotels, Playas del Este).*

◆ **Tennis** – You'll find tennis courts at the **Blau Club Arenal,** the **Villa Los Pinos** and the **Club Atlántico Hotel** *(see Hotels, Playas del Este).*

BEST BEACHES

Eastern Beaches★

Described west to east. The little cove at the mouth of the Río Bacuranao announces its beach, **Playa Bacuranao,** with its solitary hotel, Villa Izlazul Bacuranao. About 3km/2mi farther east along the Vía Blanca, you'll see the **Ciudad de los Pioneros José Martí** (Pioneer Village), by the little beach of **Playa Tarará,** now a gated tourism complex. This institution for children combined academic and athletic facilities on one campus. Since 1986 the campus has also hosted young survivors of the Chernobyl nuclear reactor meltdown.

Beyond Playa Tarará, Vía Blanca passes four beaches spread along a 10km/6mi stretch of coastline, all offering various facilities for tourists. The sands dunes of **Playa el Mégano** continue westward as far as **Playa Santa María del Mar★★,** a favored, low-key spot for international tourists, many of them Italians. A small cluster of low-to-medium-rise hotels make up the resort at Santa María. The Atlántico is the only one on the beach. Some of the Villa Los Pinos villas are close to the beach. The remainder sit across the principal, virtually traffic-free, road, **Avenida de las Terrazas.**

Santa María's wide beach is bordered by coconut palms. Amenities at this beach include rentals of reclining chairs (2CUC/day), snorkeling gear (4CUC/day) and sea kayaks (2CUC/hour). Bars on the beach and vendors on foot sell drinks and snacks.

Vía Blanca then crosses the Itabo River. On the far side of the mouth of the river lies **Playa Boca Ciega,** usually frequented by Cuban families, followed by **Guanabo★,** a popular vacation spot for vacationing Cubans, despite the brown-sand beach.

In Guanabo, Avenida 5 is lined with shops, eateries and ice-cream parlors. At the intersection of Calle 504 and Avenida 5, the small Guanabo **municipal museum** *(7 96 6647; open Mon–Fri 9am–*

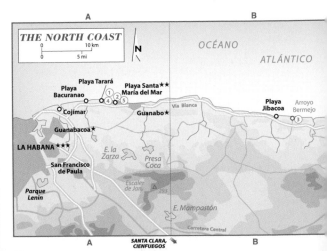

4pm, Sat 9am–noon) is devoted mostly to natural history. The organization offers guided tours at the area's nature preserves, bays and lagoons where keen observers can spot about 70 recorded species of birds *(own transportation required)*.

From the Eastern Beaches to Matanzas★

About 3km/2mi east of Guanabo, oil wells dot the Vía Blanca all the way to Santa Cruz del Norte. Before the Revolution, the French built a power plant on the coastline here. As you exit Santa Cruz you'll see a **Havana Club** rum distillery. Some 6km/4mi east of the distillery, a road to the right leads to **Playa Jibacoa,** famous for its coral reefs. Jibacoa attracts mainly Cubans, but also some Italian tourist groups. The all-inclusive resort Super-Club Breezes *(see Hotels, Playas del Este)*, situated between the hills and the beach, is popular with North American tourists. Hikes in the hills are lovely here.

Touring Tip

Don't leave personal belongings unattended on the beach. Bring sunscreen, a hat and insect repellant, although insects are not a major problem in Cuba. There are lifeguards at most beaches in high season. There are no public toilets in Santa María del Mar; visitors have to use hotel facilities.

At 20km/12mi east of Jibacoa, Vía Blanca leaves Havana Province and crosses the **Bacunayagua bridge** into Matanzas Province. The bridge, the highest in Cuba at 110 m/360ft, overlooks the **Yumuri Valley★**, a veritable garden of Eden carpeted with Royal palms; from here the **views★** of the ocean to the left and the valley to the right are excellent, particularly at sunset. The road leads to the town of **Matanzas★** *(see Best Excursions)*, some 20km/12mi beyond the bridge.

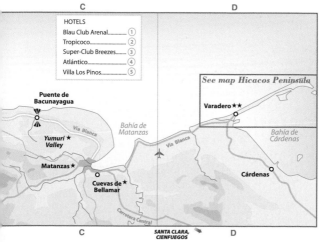

HOTELS
Blau Club Arenal .... ①
Tropicoco .... ②
Super-Club Breezes .... ③
Atlántico .... ④
Villa Los Pinos .... ⑤

Puente de Bacunayagua

See map Hicacos Peninsula

Varadero ★★

Bahía de Matanzas

Vía Blanca

Vía Blanca

Bahía de Cárdenas

Yumuri ★ Valley

Matanzas ★

Cuevas de ★ Bellamar

Cárdenas

Carretera Central

SANTA CLARA, CIENFUEGOS

BEST BEACHES

BEST EXCURSIONS

Havana is not far from attractions that appeal to beach loungers, culture lovers and ecotourists. Varadero, a popular oceanside resort with luxury and medium-priced hotels, lies 140km/87mi east of the city. En route Matanzas, alternately nicknamed the "Athens of Cuba," is a down-to-earth old town that contrasts with Varadero's modernity. Southwest of Havana, Las Terrazas offers a totally different environment, sitting as it does within a UNESCO Biosphere Reserve. A car, taxi or the Víazul bus will get you to all three; tours to these areas take the hassle out of transportation arrangements.

🚗 VARADERO★★

Lying 140km/87mi east of Havana, this year-round destination for sunbathers and snorkelers covers the entire **Hicacos Peninsula** *(see map p 102-103)*, which is named for the shrubs that flourish here. Separated from the mainland by the Paso Malo lagoon, this narrow finger of land (20km/12mi long and a third of a mile wide) extends out between the Straits of Florida and Cárdenas Bay.

Long beaches of fine, silvery white sand stretch along the northern side all the way to Las Morlas. Loudspeakers at the resorts blast music all day; parties take place nightly in most of the hotels. Quieter beaches can be found close to the town side, at the western end of the peninsula. The beaches and grand resort hotels are the main attractions, but visitors can also enjoy browsing through the markets of **Varadero town** itself, and seeing the handful of original ramshackle buildings.

Sun-washed streets are lined with sizable stone or wood villas (now small town hotels) that bear witness to the wealth of their former owners. The tip of the peninsula remains a semi-undeveloped wilderness, but hibiscus plants and other tropical vegetation are gradually being overtaken by yet more tourist-oriented vacation resorts.

Beach and Du Pont Mansion, Hicacos Peninsula

MUST SEE

Practical Information

Getting There

♦ **By Bus** – **Omnibus Interprovincial Bus Station** (Map I, D2), corner of Calle 36 and Autopista Sur, *(45) 61 4886.* **Víazul** tourist buses run from Varadero to Havana four times a day: *www.viazul.com* or tourist offices.

♦ **By Boat** – On Via Blanca as it enters Varadero, **Marina Puertosol Dársena** *(45 61 4448)* (Map I, A1–2), to the left on the lagoon, has 122 boat slips with hookups for water, electricity, fuel and security.

♦ **By Taxi** – **Cubataxi** is the official company *(45 61 4444).*

Getting Around

The Autopista Sur is the main artery along the peninsula. Getting around on foot is easy in town, but you'll need transportation to explore the rest of the peninsula.

♦ **By Bus** – The **VaraderoBeach Tour** bus runs all day long throughout the downtown area along Ave. 1ra (every 30min). Tickets 5CUC, valid all day for unlimited trips.

♦ **By Taxi** – **Cubataxi** vehicles (with meters) park in front of most hotels. Fares outside the town of Varadero run about 40CUCs. Cocotaxis may be exorbitant. **Gran Car** classic car taxis are parked in the town end of Varadero (25CUC/hr).

♦ **By Carriage** – Horsedrawn carriage rides downtown are 10CUC per person per city tour.

♦ **Car Rental** – **Havanautos**, corner of Avenida 1 and Calle 8 (Map I, A2) or 31 (Map I, C1), *(45) 61 3733/4409.* **Cubacar** (Map I, B1), corner of Avenida 1 and Calle 31, *(45) 66 7029.* **Rex** (Map 1, D2), Calle 36 across from the bus station, *(45) 61 1818.* *See also www.transturvaradero.com.*

♦ **Scooter Rentals** – Scooter rentals from Transtur (Map I, B1), corner of Avenidia 1 and Calle 21 or corner of Calle 13 and Avenida 1; and at many hotels. 12CUC/2 hours to 15CUC/ half a day and 25CUC/day.

Visitor Information

♦ **Tourist information** – **Cubanacán** (Map 1, B1), corner of Avenida 1 and Calle 23, *(45) 66 7748, wwwcubanacan.cu.* **Infotur,** Centro Commercial Hicacos, Avenida 1 between 44 and 46 and at Avenida 1 and Calle 13.

♦ **Tourist Assistance** – **Asistur** (Map I, D1, *corner of Avenida 1 and Calle 42, Edificio Marbella, 4th floor, (45) 66 7277; closed Sun*) acts as the representative for foreign insurance companies in Cuba and offers aid to international travelers, including help with lost documents, hospital admission and repatriation. Legal and financial assistance also available. 24-hour emergency assistance line: *(7) 866 8339 or 866 8527.*

♦ **Accommodations/Dining** – *see Restaurants and Hotels.*

♦ **Banks/Currency exchange** – **Banco Financiero Internacional** (Map I, C1), *Avenida 1 and Calle 32.* **Banco de Crédito y Comercio** (Map I, D1), Avenida 1 between Calles 35 and 36. **Plaza América,** KM 11 Autopista. All will cash travelers' checks, and allow you to withdraw funds in convertible pesos with a Visa card. Euros are accepted. Currency exchange desks are located in most hotels.

♦ **Health** – Visitors in need of medical aid should go to the **Clínica Internacional** (Map I, F2), corner of Avenida 1 and Calle 61; *(45) 66 7711;* there's also a 24-hour pharmacy. Some hotels have infirmaries and medical services.

Sports and Leisure

• **Water Sports** – Your hotel should offer organized water sports, or inquire at the addresses below.
Centro Internacional de Buceo Barracuda corner of Avenida 1 and Calle 59, *(45) 61 3481; www.nautica marlin.com* is Varadero's diving specialist. Barracuda is affiliated with **Acua** *(45 66 8063)* and **Marina Chapelín Diving Center** *45 66 8871*. About 50CUC for 1 dive.
Kite-surfing and **windsurfing** are also available through the Barracuda dive center *(above)*. The peninsula's three marinas offer various types of organized boat trips (catamaran,

speedboat) **Fishing** trips are available at high tide.
Marina Chapelín, *45 66 7550* offers catamaran rentals (around 300CUC for one day).
Boat Adventure (at the marina) organizes jet-ski and boat trips (2hrs). About 41CUC/person including drinks and hotel pickup. It offers a Seafari day-long cruise with snorkeling, drinks and lunch.
• **Golf** – **Varadero Golf Club**, Mansión Xanadú *(see Hotels, Varadero)*, 45 66 8482; *www.varaderogolfclub.com*. 18-hole course; lessons available.

The Resort Town

Varadero is a full-size international enclave on Cuban soil. You'll certainly meet more Canadians and Europeans than Cubans due to the cost of staying at an all-inclusive hotel. Overall, the atmosphere seems artificial because there is no real Cuban cultural experience. All bands are

imported to entertain vacationers. Most Cubans who work at the hotels are bussed in.
The town of Varadero lies between the lake at the western end named Laguna Paso Malo and Calle 64. *Avenidas* (parallel to the beach) intersect with *calles* (numbered from 1 to 64) in a standard grid-like pattern, which makes it easy

HOTELS			
Acuazul ①	Delfines (Los) ⑦	Pullman ⑤
Club Kawama ②	Dos Mares ④	Villa Tortuga ⑧
Cuatro Palmas ③	Herradura ⑥	

Museo Municipal, Varadero

©Claire Boobbyer/Michelin

for newcomers to find their way. Most stores and services catering to tourists are concentrated on the two main avenues, **Avenida Primera** and **Avenida Playa.**

Retiro Josone
Avenida 1 (Primera), between Calles 55 and 58.
This former country retreat of a wealthy Basque native who managed the Arrechabala rum factory includes a 9ha/22acre park. The tropical oasis of palm trees is nice for biking or strolling, unless you prefer to row around its artificial lake. Four restaurants are located within the park *(see Restaurants, Varadero).*

Museo Municipal
◗ *Leaving Retiro Josone from its north side, follow Calle 57 to the beachfront to reach the museum.*
This blue and white wooden mansion is home to Varadero's town museum *(open daily 10am–7pm; 1CUC).*

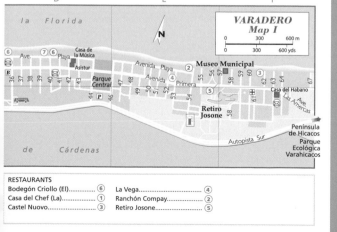

RESTAURANTS

Bodegón Criollo (El)	⑥	La Vega	④
Casa del Chef (La)	①	Ranchón Compay	②
Castel Nuovo	③	Retiro Josone	⑤

BEST EXCURSIONS

Copies of rock paintings and pottery shards, mostly found at the Cueva de Ambrosio site *(see below)*, give insight into the life of now extinct Siboney Indians. The building is a typical Varadero house. Its terrace, with a view of the sea, opens up onto a garden planted with *uvas caletas,* the local name of the ornamental sea-grape.

🏝 Hicacos Peninsula

Driving Tour; about 2hrs by car.

Luxury resorts have been spreading towards Punta Morlas, the easternmost part of Varadero. At the western entrance to Varadero, the Autopista Sur takes over from the Via Blanca as the major highway continuing east.

◐ *Follow Avenida 1 east out of town onto the Autopista del Sur. After about 4km/2mi, take a left at the signpost.*

Mansión Du Pont de Nemours (Mansión Xanadú)

Built in 1930 for the French-born chemical magnate **Francis Irénée Du Pont de Nemours**, the mansion derives its better known name of **Xanadú** from Samuel Taylor Coleridge's poem hanging on one of its walls. Overlooking turquoise waters from the San Bernardino crags, the extravagant 4-story mansion was once the centerpiece of a huge estate that included its own golf course, private beach, and gardens planted with coconut trees, flowers and vegetables. Turned into a boutique hotel *(see Hotels)*, the former Du Pont family residence now offers guests a refined interior that measures up to the magnificent outdoor setting. Take in views of the coastline while sipping a cocktail in the top-floor bar to the backdrop of live jazz and Cuban traditional music, or dine in the Xanadú restaurant *(see Restaurants, Varadero).*

◐ *Get back on Autopista Sur, and drive north 5km/2.5mi.*

Delfinario

This facility presents **dolphin shows** *(daily 9:30am–5pm; 15CUC)* and opportunities to swim with dolphins in the lagoon *(reservations only; 89CUC/person).*

◐ *Continue north on Autopista Sur to a sign on the left of the highway pointing to Cueva Ambrosio.*

Cueva Ambrosio

Open daily 9am–4:30pm. 34CUC.
Discovered in 1961, this cave is decorated with red and black rock paintings from the pre-Hispanic period. Some of the drawings lend credence to the theory that runaway

PENÍNSULA DE HICACOS
Map II

0   2 km
0   1 mi

N

★★ Varadero
See map 1
VARADERO

Matanzas
Playas del Este
La Habana

Vía Blanca

Cárdenas

Isla del Sur

slaves may have found refuge here. The cave is located in the **Parque Ecológico Varahicacos,** a still pristine coastal lagoon surrounded by woodland. This large protected area is known for its coastal birds (both local and migratory), and traces of ancient humans.

○ *Continue to the next intersection.*

Punta Hicacos Sector
Parque Ecológico Varahicacos. Open daily 9am–4:30pm. www.varahicacos.cu.
In this part of the Área Protegida Varahicacos, **guided walks** *(3CUC)* along the park's interpretive trails allow visitors to discover some of its highlights: Cueva Ambrosio *(opposite)*; the **Cuevas Musulmanes,** a 2,000-year-old burying site of 19C Cuban smugglers calling themselves "Moslems"; and a 500-year-old giant cactus called **El Patriarca. Playa las Calaveras,** a beautiful beach opening onto the Straits of Florida, can also be accessed from the park.

○ *Return to Varadero via the Autopista Sur.*

DAY TRIP TO
🏖 MATANZAS★

○ *42km/26mi west of Varadero.*
By Bus: The MatanzasBusTour travels to and from Varadero. By Car/Taxi: Take the Autopista Sur west to Vía Blanca, which runs through the northeast part of Matanzas. At the waterfront, Vía Blanca turns right and becomes Calle 61. Take a right onto Calle 61, cross the Río Yumurí and continue three blocks.

Divided by the Yumurí and San Juan rivers, Matanzas (meaning "slaughter") was founded in 1693 on the site of an old slaughterhouse.

The Town
Once a wealthy colonial town with a lively intellectual and cultural life, Matanzas remains an active port, but at a reduced level of activity.

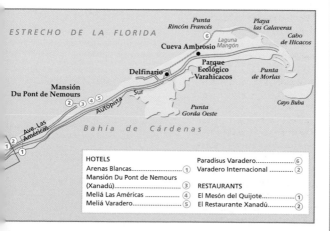

HOTELS	
Arenas Blancas	①
Mansión Du Pont de Nemours (Xanadú)	③
Meliá Las Américas	④
Meliá Varadero	⑤
Paradisus Varadero	⑥
Varadero Internacional	②
RESTAURANTS	
El Mesón del Quijote	①
El Restaurante Xanadú	②

Bacunayagua bridge to Matanzas

©Claire Boobbyer/Michelin

There are two attractions definitely worth seeing in the historic center. On the outskirts of town, the Bellamar Caves are a draw for visitors to the area.

Teatro Sauto★★
○ *East side of the Plaza de la Vigía.*
Visit by guided tour daily 9am–5pm; 2CUC.
This Neoclassical building (1863) was designed by Italian Daniele dell'Aglio, who painted the exquisite **ceiling★★** in the main hall. French actress Sarah Bernhardt performed here in 1887 and Russian ballerina Anna Pavlova in 1915.

Museo Farmacéutico★★★
Calle 83, south of Plaza de la Libertad, four blocks from Teatro Sauto. Open Mon–Sat 10am–5pm, Sun 9am–2pm. 3CUC.
This pink building with a wrought-iron balcony houses an antique pharmacy founded in 1882 by a Frenchman who married into a respected Cuban family of pharmacists. Remarkably restored, the old store features porcelain jars imported from France, a bronze scale, and other curiosities. In the former **laboratory,** behind the inner courtyard, are a still, a cauldron and copper instruments.

🕳 Cuevas de Bellamar★ (Bellamar Caves)

○ *3km/2mi southeast of Matanzas.*

By Car/Taxi: From Plaza de la Vigía in Matanzas, cross the Calixto García bridge and proceed on Calle 272 for about a quarter of a mile. Turn right in front of the bus terminal. The caves are sign-posted to your left at the next intersection. Open daily 9:30am–5pm. 5CUC. Guided tours (1hr) available. Two restaurants on-site.
These caves were discovered in the mid-19C by a farm laborer. The 3km/2mi of galleries open to the public are actually part of a much larger cave system. Pure crystal formations include **crystal lamps** and natural limestone concretions bearing evocative names like Columbus' Cloak and Chapel of the Twelve Apostles. A **museum** details the geology of these submarine caves.

🕳 LAS TERRAZAS★

Map inside back cover.
○ *75km/47mi southwest of Havana by the Autopista.*
Víazul bus stops twice a day; 6CUC. Entrance fee 4CUC. www.lasterrazas.cu.

Located in western Artemisa province, Las Terrazas (Spanish for "terraces") is possibly the best and most developed

ecotourism project in Cuba. This rural community (population 1,000) is part of the **Sierra del Rosario,** a designated UNESCO Biosphere Reserve encompassing a 26,686ha/103sq mi area of protected rivers, valleys and mountains that was cleared of natural forest by cattle ranches and coffee and tobacco plantations. The degradation of the land left local farmers impoverished. In the late 1960s, a development plan for the Sierra region was launched involving terracing 5,000ha/19sq mi of hills that had been stripped of vegetation, and reforesting them to stop erosion. Decades later, the Sierra's forests are showing signs of regeneration. The **Las Terrazas Tourism Complex** (1994), an eco-resort that is testament to the success of sustainable tourism, overlooks the village's attractive white houses cascading down to Lake San Juan.

Hotel Moka

In Las Terrazas. Reservations through the hotel's office in Havana, or online. (7) 204 3739. www.lasterrazas.cu.

Beautifully sited high above the valley, Hotel Moka is one of the country's loveliest hotels. An example of organic architecture, the building is linear in shape, and matches the contours of the hill on which it was built. Its whitewashed walls and red-tile roof reflect the style of Las Terrazas' local houses and bungalows.
Trees were integrated into the overall design (one soars through the roof of the hotel's lobby, for instance), and large bathrooms' windows invite the outdoors in.

Spacious, well decorated rooms offer all the conveniences. Rooms on the lower level provide a plunging view over the lake. A few rustic cabins can be found 3km/2mi west of the hotel, next to the Río San Juan. Rooms are available in some of the local homes around the lake *(www.lasterrazas.cu/_english/ dondedormir.htm).*

Activities

Shopping – Artisans and artists' studios present a wide range of techniques, from fiber and weaving art to silk-screen printing. Daily 9am–5pm (Sat–Sun til noon).
Canopy ride – 900m/2,952ft zip wire *(15CUC Hotel Moka guests, 25CUC nonguests).*
Hiking – Marked **trails** in the Sierra del Rosario are dotted with waterfalls, natural pools and vestiges of old coffee plantations. Contact Hotel Moka for tours. About 2km/1.2mi northeast of Las Terrazas, on Las Delicias hill, hikers can take a tour around the partly restored **Buenavista coffee plantation;** its coffee-drying area is equipped with antique machinery.
All around you, note impressive *almácigos,* commonly known as "tourist trees" because of their red, peeling bark. The on-site restaurant serves Creole cuisine.

OUTDOOR LIFE

Thanks to Ernest Hemingway, Cuba is known for its superb sport fishing. Because of its pristine coral reefs, the country is also a popular diving destination. Opportunities for golf, horseback riding, hiking and other outside pursuits can be found in or near Havana. As for spectator sports, baseball reigns supreme as the national pastime, but domino games run a close second with boxing. Be sure to build some time into your trip to enjoy a few sports activities. You'll have fun and learn about the Cuban psyche in the process.

Activity Sports

Situated along the sea and enjoying year-round sunshine, Havana and outlying areas hold several opportunities to partake of the Great Outdoors.

Most leisure activities for visitors are organized by the international hotels. However, you can escape the official circuit on occasion and participate in the same type of activities via private individuals. The biggest delight for unsuspecting enthusiasts may be encounters like an excursion on the fishing boat with local boatmen.

Boating

The large seaside hotels often organize day-long trips out to sea. Participants take the boat in the morning to a *cayo* (a key or low-lying island) where they spend the day. Lunch is normally included in the price of the excursion.

Marina Hemingway (Map 1) offers a complete range of aquatic sports, such as deep-sea fishing, diving, snorkeling and sailing. Charter boats and excursions can be booked. *Calle 248 and Avenida 5. (7) 204 6847. www.nauticamarlin.com.*

Diving

Surrounded by innumerable coral reefs, Cuba presents ample opportunities for snorkeling and deep-sea diving. Most all of the seaside resorts offer instruction for both beginners and proficient divers. You can make a dive on your own for about 35CUC (often

Sailing a catamaran, Varadero

©Claire Boobbyer/Michelin

Fishing on the Malecón

several combined dives will be offered at a lower price) or pursue your international ACUC training (equivalent to PADI). Marina Hemingway *(above)* has a dive center, and most of the diving centers offer international certification as well as special dives (night dives, diving in caves, deep dives, etc.). The price runs between 200CUC and 400CUC, depending on the dive chosen.

It is also possible to rent a diving mask and a snorkel for less than 5CUC. You can organize your diving visit via a specialized tour operator *(see Practical Information)* or at Marina Hemingway. The dry season (November-April) offers the best visibility for diving.

Fishing

Fishing enthusiasts can pursue their hobby in either fresh water or saltwater. The best seasons for fishing (marlin, swordfish) are spring and summer.

Several ocean tournaments are organized during this period, of which the most famous, the International Hemingway

Tournament, is in June *(see Calendar of Events)* at the Marina Hemingway *(see above)*. The island also has a number of fresh water lakes that abound with trout; in winter, the trout reach their largest size. Find out about conditions from Infotur or your hotel before you go, because the lakes may dry up in summer.

Golf

Cuba is far from being a golfer's paradise, but there are a few fairways in the Havana area. The **Club de Golf Habana**—also known as the Diplomatic Golf Club, since it was formed by British diplomats in the 1920s—is a 9-hole course located off Carratera Vento *(KM 8 Capdevila, Rancho Boyeras; 7 649 8918)*, 9km/5mi south of the Plaza de la Revolución on the way to the airport. The 18-hole course at **Varadero** lies next to the Dupont de Nemours mansion *(see Best Excursions)*. Equipment rental and caddy hires are available at both courses. Infotur or your hotel excursion desk can help you with reservations.

OUTDOOR LIFE

109

Golfing at Varadero

©Abel Ernesto/Michelin

🏊 Hiking

The Infotur/tour operator offices located at many of Havana's larger hotels can help organize nature hikes in the outlying areas. The **Sierra del Rosario,** for example, has several marked trails leading to waterfalls, swimming holes and remains of old coffee plantations *(see Best Excursions, Las Terrazas).* Only guided tours are permitted, however. The **Area Protegida Varahicacos** offers interpretive trails on the Hicacos Peninsula *(see Best Excursions, Varadero).*

🎾 Tennis

Seaside resort clubs often have tennis courts. Club Habana (formerly the Havana Biltmore Yacht & Country Club, founded in 1928) has tennis courts that may be used by nonmembers for a fee *(Avenida 5 between Calles 188 and 192, Playa; 7 204 3300; www.cpalco.com).* Club de Golf Habana *(see Golf, above)* has five courts, and nonmember passes may be purchased for the day. Racquets can be rented and tennis balls purchased.

Water Sports

With its lengthy coastline, the area east of Havana is a 🏊 **swimmer's paradise**. The crystalline waters of the eastern beaches *(see Playas Del Este)* and the beaches off Varadero and the Hicacos Peninsula *(see Best*

Hiking, Sierra del Rosario

©Claire Boobbyer/Michelin

Excursions) maintain temperatures of 79°F sto 82°F year-round; many of these beaches have lifeguards in front of the international hotels. A diving mask may be useful to avoid the occasional jelly fish along the coast.

The big seaside hotels offer international visitors a range of aquatic sports: sail boarding, diving, **snorkeling** and **catamaran sailing**. In the clubs offering *todo incluido,* the renting of gear and equipment, except motorized equipment, is included in the price of your stay.

Spectator Sports

Baseball

Cubans excel at baseball, the national sport, and consistently take first place in international tournaments. Baseball fans can attend a game at Havana's stadium for the National Series teams, **Estadio Latinoamericano** (Map IV, B3) *302 Calle Pedro Pérez, between Calles Patria and Sarabia, in Cerro, southeast of the Plaza de la Revolución; 7 870 6526 ext 29 or 870-2677*. Your hotel can most likely make arrangements for you. The season runs from November to June. To see local residents playing the game, all you need to do is visit a public square or park. Armed with a bat and a glove too big for their hands, Havana's youth tirelessly imitate the moves of their favorite baseball stars.

Boxing

A source of national pride, boxing has become a topic of a good number of local conversations, though boxing definitely takes second place to baseball *(beisbol*

or *pelota)* on the island. Habaneros comment ceaselessly about the accomplishments of their athletes in baseball and boxing.

During international competitions, Cuba often places first among countries in Latin America and elsewhere. Since the 1972 Olympics, Cuban boxers have continued to distinguished themselves, taking the gold, silver and bronze medals consistently in this amateur sport, with only a couple of exceptions.

In Old Havana the **Arena Rafael Trejo** *(815 Calle Cuba, between Calles Merced and Leonor Pérez)*, where boxers train, is open to the public *(admission fee)*. International matches are generally held at Havana's **Ciudad Deportiva** *(Via Blanca and Boyeros, in Cerro; 7 648 7047)*.

Dominoes

Cuban men occasionally gather around a card table, or even a doorstep, for long sessions of dominoes, the island's national game. From time to time they may make miraculous moves that keep the game going throughout the evening and sometimes even until dawn.

Several places in Havana consistently draw domino players—and spectators—usually the public **city parks**, such as Parque Central. Watch for men concentrating over tables in most any of Havana's parks, large and small *(see Parks and Gardens)*.

PERFORMING ARTS

Happily, Havana's grand theaters and performance spaces are still humming today with music, dance and drama. An evening of culture is possible several nights of the week, especially during one of the city's many festivals *(see Calendar of Events)*. Havana is home to Cuba's world-class national ballet company and the national symphony orchestra. You may have an opportunity to watch performances by international groups as well as Cuban actors, singers, dancers and musicians. Listings of weekly and monthly cultural offerings can be found at *www.cubaabsolutely*.com and *www.cubanow.net*, both in English, and *http://habana.kewelta.cu (in Spanish)*.

Ballet and Opera

Gran Teatro Habana
Off Parque Central, between Calles San José and San Rafael, La Habana Vieja. (7) 861 3077. This historic building *(see Cuban Classics)* hosts performances by the country's national ballet company, the **Ballet Nacional de Cuba,** under the direction of nonagenarian Alicia Alonso *(see Museums)*. Founded right after the Revolution, the internationally renowned national ballet has performed its repertoire of classic ballets such as *Coppélia, Giselle, The Nutcracker* and *Swan Lake* for local audiences as well as those abroad in the US, in Latin America and in other countries. The theater also serves as the primary venue for Havana's International Ballet Festival held biennially *(see Calendar of Events)*.

Teatro Lírico Nacional
253 Calle Zulueta, between Calles Animas and Neptuno, La Habana Vieja. (7) 860-1511, ext. 110. Cuba's **National Opera Company** practices zarzuelas and operas that are then staged in the Sala García Lorca at the Gran Teatro Habana *(weekends, most months; 25CUC)*. Every weekend, the company give concerts *(5CUC)* at 5pm at the Zulueta location *(address above)*.

Ballet Nacional de Cuba

©Abel Ernesto/Michelin

MUST DO

Teatro Nacional

BOX OFFICE

©Claire Boobbyer/Michelin

Classical Music

Teatro National

Corner of Avenida Paseo and Calle 39, off the Plaza de la Revolución, Vedado. (7) 078 5590/ 870 4655. www.teatronacional.cult.cu (in Spanish).

On occasion you can attend concerts by the **National Symphony Orchestra** *(see Teatro Amadeo Roldán opposite)* at the Teatro National (Map IV). Constructed in 1959, this imposing Modern-style building houses the National Theater of Cuba. It features a glass-wall façade and large glass-wall overhang. The interior comprises two large rooms, the 2,500-seat Sala Avellaneda and 850-seat Sala Covarrubias, both with excellent acoustics.

The theater has been installed with up-to-date lighting and sound systems. Its backstage facilities include costume storage, makeup rooms, and special effects staging areas.

On the 9th floor, **Piso 9** is a warehouse converted to a stage for productions of cutting-edge drama and dance. In the basement, Café Cantante specializes in salsa nights, and on the third floor is the popular piano bar Delirio Habanero *(see Landmarks with a Beat)*.

Teatro Amadeo Roldán

Corner of Avenida 7 and Calle D, Vedado. Performances Tue 8:30pm, Fri and Sat 5pm, Sun 6pm. (7) 832-1168.

Classical music concerts are held here at the Teatro Amadeo Roldán (Map IV, A1). This theater serves as the home base for Cuba's **National Symphony Orchestra,** founded in 1959. The orchestra goes on regularly scheduled world tours, performing in Latin America, Russia and Europe. Over the years, it has made several recordings, and plays at the annual International Ballet Festival in Havana. Program listings are posted in the lobby.

Teatro Karl Marx

Calle 1 and Calle 10, Miramar. (7) 203 0801.

Teatro Karl Marx is Havana's largest performance space: its auditorium seats more than 5,000 people. The

existing theater was renamed in 1959 for the German philosopher Karl Marx (1818-1883), known for his socio-economic theory called Marxism. Classical concerts are performed here as well as drama productions and rock concerts. Its cafe is a popular meeting spot.

Teatro América
253 Calle Galiano, at the corner of Calle Concordia, Centro Habana.
This theater *(see Cuban Classics)* is used less for classical concerts than for the staging of shows, cabaret and, on Thursdays, comedians. Traditional Cuban music and jazz are usually presented on weekends *(Fri, Sat & Sun; 5CUC).*

Dance

Conjunto Folklórico Nacional de Cuba
103 Calle 4, between Calzada and Avenida 5, Vedado. (7) 830 3939. www.folkcuba.cult.cu.
The country's Afro-Cuban dance heritage is kept alive by a number

Conjunto Folklórico Nacional de Cuba

of groups, most notably by the Conjunto Folklórico Nacional, founded in 1962. Over the years the ensemble has thrilled international audiences in the US, Russia, Africa, Europe and Latin America during its world tours. Their colorful and sometimes outlandish costumes as well as their infectious rhythms, primarily from Cuban percussion instruments, make their productions a must-see experience.
Based in Havana, at **El Gran Palenque** in Vedado *(see address),* they regularly put on shows there

Danza Contemporánea de Cuba

and in the **Teatro Mella** *(657 Linea, between Calle A and B, Vedado)*. Their performances are open to the public, and the group maintains a biannual schedule of lessons in Afro-Cuban dance and music for the public *(see website)*.

Danza Contemporánea de Cuba

www.dccuba.com.

The Contemporary Dance Company of Cuba, created in 1959, presents its own unique form of modern dance with a decidedly Cuban flavor.

Widely praised, the award-winning group performs primarily at the National Theater *(see above)*, but occasionally stages their productions at other venues like the Gran Teatro de la Habana *(see above)*. It tours abroad as well, so you will need to be on the look-out for listings for its Cuba dates. Classes are taught to children and adults through Cubadanza twice a year. See the website for details.

Asociación Cultura Yoruba de Cuba

615 Prado, between Calles Monte and Dragones, La Habana Vieja. (7) 863 5953. www.cuba yoruba.cult.cu.

Folkloric dancing takes place here Thursdays and Sundays between 5pm and 8pm. *Tambores* are ceremonies that honor the *orishas* *(see p94)* using the ritual drums of Santería, called the batáa. The *fiestas de santo* are dedicated to individual *orishas*. They take place at 4pm on the day divined for the celebration. It is best to call beforehand to see if the date has been determined by the *orisha*.

Drama

Teatro Nacional *(see above)* often books actors and actresses from overseas to perform traditional and contemporary plays for Cuban and international audiences. Teatro Nacional's **Piso 9**, on the 9th floor, is reserved for workshops and cutting-edge theater and dance.

The annual **Festival de Teatro de La Habana** at the end of October/beginning of November is held at venues across the city. Consult *www.cubaescena.cult.cu* for information. More useful for regularly held events is *www.cubaabsolutely.com.*

In Vedado, venues to pay attention to are the Sala Hubert de Blanck *(Calzada 657 between A and B)*, the **Teatro El Sótano** *(Calle K between 25 and 27)*, and the **Teatro Trianón** *(Línea between Paseo and A)*. The latter is host to the Teatro El Público, which stages conventional and avant-garde theater.

Puppet Shows

The Havana area boasts two puppet theaters: in Vedado, **Teatro Guiñol** *(Calle M, between Calles 17 and 19; 7 832 6262)* and in La Habana Vieja, a new shadow puppet theater, **Teatro-Museo de Títeres El Arca,** has opened at *Avenida del Puerto and Calle Obrapía (7 864 8953)*.

BOX OFFICE

PERFORMING ARTS

SHOPPING

As the capital of Cuba, Havana offers a shopping experience that is varied compared to the rest of the island. Outdoor crafts and vegetable markets, government-run chains, museum shops, hotel boutiques and street vendors present a limited array of choices for visitors, but merchandise is not plentiful or bargain-priced. What's missing? Consumerism is absent on a large scale. There are no Western-modeled megamalls—but most visitors don't come to Havana to shop in a mall. There are a couple of basic shopping centers in La Habana Vieja, but it's the individual shops and open-air markets in quaint neighborhoods that are the draw for most tourists.

Before You Buy

Opening Hours – Outdoor markets are usually open daily from 10am to 5pm. Most stores are open Monday through Saturday 10am to 6pm, and closed Sunday. Hotel boutiques and souvenir shops are generally open daily until 7pm.

Public Conveniences – Other than hotels, some stores have public restrooms. Toilet paper is often in short supply, so best to bring your own.

Taxes and Regulations – There is no sales tax in Cuba. Check Customs regulations in your home country with regard to alcohol and tobacco to avoid having your items confiscated at the border. Art galleries must provide you with a receipt for all purchases; otherwise you'll need to acquire a special certificate allowing you to transport goods out of Cuba. There's a kiosk in the Almacenes San José crafts market for processing these certificates.

Bargaining

The custom of bargaining for lower prices at the crafts market is relatively new in Cuba, appearing along with the advent of tourism. Prices are fixed in state-run businesses, but might be subject

Souvenirs at Havana market

to negotiation for better rates in private-sector operations such as rooms in private homes, or privately operated taxis. Outside tourism zones you'll find few merchants willing to bargain hard, even though their prices may be exorbitant, thanks to a lack of competition.

Shipping Your Purchases

It's always best to simply bring items you've purchased in Cuba with you in your carry-on or checked luggage. If you absolutely must ship your purchases, use an express service such as **DHL**. Such services can be expensive, but it's the only way to be certain your belongings will arrive safely and quickly. When time and security are of the essence, send packages by DHL express service. A DHL counter can be found on Calzada between Calles 2 and 4 in Vedado, and at the corner of Avenida 1 and Calle 26 in Miramar (Map V, B1).

Cuban Specialties

Crafts

The burgeoning role of tourism in Cuba's economy has given rise to a cottage industry of handicrafts that, while produced here, don't spring from any long Cuban tradition. In tourist areas throughout Havana you'll invariably find wooden statues, carved coconuts, necklaces, palm hats, and little dolls representing the divinities of Santería—all rather commonplace souvenirs.

Cigars

Every cigar aficionado will tell you: Havana cigars are like fine French wines. The creation of

excellent cigars is an elaborate art, and the ability to truly appreciate their subtleties takes time and experience. If you're new to cigar smoking, there's not much to be gained by starting with a complex type such as a Cohiba (the best of the best); the nuances of taste will be lost on a beginner, and it won't be worth the extremely high price (around 460CUCs for a box of 25). It's best to buy a variety of single cigars so you can compare how they look, feel and taste before investing in a box of your favorite. Store your purchases in a specially made humidor or box designed to maintain humidity and temperature for proper aging.

SHOPPING

The Art of Buying Cigars

When you buy a cigar, check the quality of the exterior wrapper leaf; avoid those with thick ribs or veins. The wrapper leaf itself should be thick and slightly oily. A dark black wrapper *(oscuro)* indicates a cigar with a very strong flavor; if you're just beginning, stick with a lighter, tan shade of wrapper *(claro)* or medium brown *(colorado-claro)*.

The particularities of a cigar's aroma and taste come from its **filler**, composed of three separate types of tobacco; the *ligero* (source of its taste); the *volado* (for burning) and the *seco* (aroma and strength). It's the combination of these three tobaccos that gives a cigar its particular flavor and aroma, and each major cigar brand his its own characteristic blend.

©Sylvaine Poitau/Apa Publications

The choice of cigar type is also very important, as size and diameter greatly affect the smoker's experience. A 12cm Corona will be quite a different smoke than a Montecristo A, which measures 24cm long and 1.9cm in diameter. The **time of day** should also dictate the selection of an appropriate cigar; for example, the **Romeo y Julieta** Corona is light and woody, perfect for after lunch. A Churchill or a Prince of Wales (also by Romeo y Julieta) are better in the evening. Morning, after coffee, is the best time to indulge in a smaller **Partagás** Corona, but the Corona made by **Juan López** or the Small Club by **Ramon Allones** are recommended for mid-day. Try the Royal Corona made by **Bolivar** after a light meal; it's a good, characteristically Cuban cigar. The **Rey del Mundo** Choix Supreme and the **Monterrey** Epicure No. 2 are also good choices for newer smokers making their first forays into the complicated world of Cuban cigars.

Quality cigars can be purchased in most Casa del Habano branches or in shops in major hotels. Beware of resellers offering cigars at low prices; their quality is often inferior and the lack of a proper receipt will likely cause problems with Customs *(see PRACTICAL INFORMATION)*. *Never buy cigars on the street; they will not be authentic, and you could end up spending your money on nothing more than banana leaves.*

Rum

There's a good chance that a bottle or two of famed Cuban rum will be joining the cigars in your suitcase. Good choices for rum novices include 3-year-old white rum *(Carta Blanca)*, excellent for use in mixed drinks. For aficionados, 5-year-old light rum *(Carta de Oro)* or Añejo, a dark rum aged 7 years, are ideal for drinking dry or on the rocks. Depending on the brand, expect to pay anywhere from 4CUC to 90CUC for a bottle. You'll find rum by **Havana Club** for sale everywhere in Cuba, but there are other excellent national brands.

Other Products

Art

Art galleries mount shows and handle sales of contemporary Cuban paintings and sculptures. Be sure to get a proper receipt to justify your purchases when passing through Customs.

Books and Curios

The selection may be quite limited in Havana bookstores, particularly for works in English. Much the same assortment of books in Spanish can be found from one bookstore to another: novels of Alejo Carpentier, essays of Fernando Ortíz, diaries of Che Guevara, poems by Nicolás Guillén, exposes of Cuban music and religion, and of course writings of Fidel Castro.

People also sometimes offer shelves of books for sale on the doorsteps of their homes or places of business. In Havana, look for book stalls in the Plaza de Armas; with diligent searching, it's possible to find a rare treasure or two. Stamps, coins, letters, brass curios and memorabilia make these stalls a must-stop for curiosity-seekers.

Clothing

You won't have any trouble finding T-shirts printed with the figure of Che Guevara, but for traditional Cuban garb, take home a *guayabera*, the pleated cotton shirt that most Cubans wear untucked over pants. Havana markets are a good place to buy blouses, skirts and scarves embellished with Cuban lace. Guayaberas can be purchased at **El Quitrín**, on the corner of Calle Obispo and Calle San Ignacio in La Habana Vieja.

Music, DVDs and Film Posters

Souvenir shops sell CDs, but the choice is often quite limited. You'll almost certainly find recordings by popular Cuban groups. Plan to spend around 6CUC for a traditional salsa recording, or around 15CUC for current pop music. The best places to source music are in the attached shops of the Casas de la Música in the city or at the helpful Habana Sí shop, corner of Calle L and 23, opposite the Tryp Habana Libre hotel. It

©Claire Boobbyer/Michelin

El Quitrín

SHOPPING

119

also sells Cuban film DVDs. The most comprehensive collection of Cuban films on DVD can be found at the shop inside **Cafe Fresa y Chocolate** (*Calle 23 between Calles 10 and 12, Vedado*). That shop also has the largest collection of film posters in the city.

Musical Instruments

Craft markets and souvenir shops are good places to find traditional Cuban percussion instruments like *maracas, congas, tumbadoras, timbales* and *makutas*. For the best selection, visit the Casa de la Música in Centro Habana and the Longina Música shop at 360 Calle Obispo in La Habana Vieja.

Drums for sale

©Claire Boobbyer/Michelin

Where to Shop

Markets

An open-air market sets up on Calle Obispo in La Habana Vieja every day of the week. Browse them to find craft objects, books, CDs and many other tourist-oriented items.

Fruits and vegetables are found at produce markets called **agromercados**. In La Habana Vieja, there is an agromercado at **La Catedral** *(Empedrado, between Monserrate and Villegas)* as well as indoors (agromercado Egido) at Egido (Avenida de Bélgica), between Calles Corrales and Apodaca. In **Vedado**, an agromercado *(open Tue–Sun)* is located at *Calle B, between Calles 17 and 19* (Map IV, A2).

Gift Shops

Tourists in Havana should seek out small *tiendas* as well as Artex gift shops; the latter is a chain specializing in traditional cultural Cuban items. You can also find gift shops in hotels and airports.

Rum, Coffee and Cigars

Casa del Ron (Map III, B2), corner of Calles Baratillo (no. 53) and Obispo (Old Havana). This famed purveyor of rum, located just behind the Plaza de Armas, offers tastings and sales of several brands of rum as well as Cuban cigars. You can also buy rum at the **Fundación Havana Club** *(p 50)* in Old Havana. Next door to the Casa del Ron, the **Casa del Café** sells every type of coffee grown in Cuba. For tasting, go upstairs to the tasting room and coffee bar on the second floor.

Fábrica Partagás (Map II, A3), *524 Calle Industria (just behind the Capitolio). Open Mon–Fri 9am–11am and 12:30pm–3pm.* You'll find a huge selection of cigars here on the ground floor of Havana's oldest cigar factory.

Casa del Habano (Map III, B2), *Calle Mercaderes between Calles Obispo and Obrapía. Open daily 10am–7pm (Sun til 5pm).* A cigar

Fábrica de Tabacos Partagás

©Claire Boobbyer/Michelin

shop like many others (most large hotels sell fine cigars), but this one dates from the 17C, with displays about the history of tobacco and the cigar-making process.

Crafts

Souvenir stands operate daily in a new covered crafts market, **Almacenes San José**, on Avenida del Puerto, close to the Iglesia San Francisco de Paula. Here, you will also find cafes, public toilets and Internet access. You'll also find

souvenir stands in the Vedado, at the intersection the La Rampa and Calle M (Map IV, B1). Expect piles of straw hats, carved coconut shells, art work, photographs, Che Guevara T-shirts, laces—a veritable catalogue of Cuban handicrafts. **Palacio de la Artesanía** (Map II, B2), in the *Palacio Pedroso, 64 Calle Cuba between Calles Peña Pobre and Tacón. Open daily 9:30am–7pm.* Just a few steps from the cathedral, in a handsome 18C house, this fine shop sells books,

Crafts market merchandise

©Claire Boobbyer/Michelin

SHOPPING

CDs, musical instruments, rum and cigars. It's a perfect spot for one-stop souvenir shopping.

El Quitrín (Map III, A2), corner of Calles Obispo and San Ignacio. This Old Havana shop is a good place to buy quality handmade laces and *guayaberas* (traditional cotton shirts) at reasonable prices.

Arte Malecón (Map IV, A1), *Calle D between Avenidas 1 and 3. Open Mon–Sat 11am–7pm, Sun 10am–2pm*. This store offers a large selection of books, music and audiovisual materials along with linens, clothing and dinnerware painted by Cuban artists.

Art Galleries

Art galleries abound in Havana, particularly in Old Havana. At *354 Prado between Calles Virtudes and Neptuno*, **Taller de Patria** (Map II, A2) *(open daily 10am–10pm)* showcases some very interesting work by young Cuban painters.

Taller Experimental de Gráfica (Map III, A2) *(open Mon–Sat 10am–4pm)*, near the cathedral, is a large printmaking studio with works for sale.

Galería La Acacia (Map II, A3), *114 Calle San José between Calles Industria and Consulado. Open Mon–Fri and every other Sat 10am–4pm*. The gallery carries works by some of Cuba's best-known artists, at commensurate (high) prices.

Galeria La Casona (Map II, C3), *corner of 107 Calles Muralla and San Ignacio, (7) 863 4703. Open Tue–Sat 9am–5pm*. Four galleries occupy this 18C palace; the most interesting one, devoted to contemporary art, is located on the floor above the patio.

Galeria Habana (Map IV, A1), *460 Calle Línea between Calles E and F, (7) 832 7101, www.galeri habana.com. Open Mon–Sat 10am–4:30pm, Sun 9am–1pm*. The best of Cuban contemporary art makes its way to this gallery, representing Rigoberta Mena, Esterio Segura, and Carlos Quintana among others.

Centro de Arte Contemporáneo Wifredo Lam (Map III, A1), *corner of Calles Ignacio and Empedrado*. Here you'll see rotating works belonging to Cuba's contemporary artists. Stop by the pleasant patio for a quick drink.

Casa de Guayasamín (Map III, B2), *Calle Obrapía between Calles Mercaderes and Oficios*. One of Ecuador's most celebrated artists (famed for his portrait of Fidel Castro) maintains his Cuban gallery here. You're welcome to peruse the sculptures, paintings, ceramics and jewelry on view. Across the street, the **Casa de México** displays art and handicrafts of Mexico.

Jacqueline Brito Jorje (Map IV), *309 Calle 6, between Calles 13 and 15 (Vedado), (05) 835 2823 (cell phone)*. Iconic works by a young Cuban painter.

Casa de las Américas (Map IV, A1), *corner of Avenida de los Presidentes and Avenida 3 (Vedado). Open Mon–Fri 10am–4pm*. Latin American cultural center with a bookshop and art exhibits.

Books

Everywhere in Havana you'll see shelves of books for sale outside doorways. Browse from one to another as the selections of one seller are often limited and quite different from another seller.

Book stalls, Plaza de Armas
©Claire Boobbyer/Michelin

Book Market (Map III, B2), *Plaza de Armas*. Open daily. A few rare finds lurk among the stacks of books by Fidel Castro, Che Guevara, Fernando Ortíiz and Nicolás Guillén. The prices marked are somewhat high; bargaining is essential.

La Internacional (Map II, A3), *526 Calle Obispo between Calles Bernaza and Cristo. Open Mon–Sat 10am-6:30pm*. Books and magazines in several languages.

🛒 Shopping Center

Centro Comercial Plaza Carlos III (Map IV, B2), *Avenida Salvador Allende (Carlos III), between Calles Retiro and Arbol Seco. Open daily 10am-6pm (Sun til 1pm)*. The opening of this large shopping center in Centro Habana was a big event. The mall boasts four floors of shops selling shoes, clothes, books, appliances and electronics among other items.

Perfume

Habana 1791, *at 156 Calle Mercaderes, at the corner of Calle Obrapía*.

🛒 Fans

Casa del Abanico, *107 Calle Obrapía, between Calles Mercaderes and Oficios. (7) 863 4452*. This new shop sells a variety of handheld fans ranging from bold and brash to delicately hand-painted ones. Customers seeking the individual touch can have their fans personalized for a small fee while they wait.

©Claire Boobbyer/Michelin
Habana 1791

NIGHTLIFE

Evening entertainment in Havana may no longer rival the city's heyday in the 1950s, when international celebrities and other VIPs flocked here for a show at the Tropicana or a drink at the bar in Hotel Nacional, but the capital still has many options for a night on the town. You can start with dinner in one of Havana's restaurants followed by an evening of bar-hopping, live jazz, salsa dancing or cabaret.

Getting Your Bearings

Many **bars** and **clubs** at hotels attract big crowds of foreigners and Cubans. The music at these hotels usually alternates between salsa and pop music.

Specific hotels organize **cabaret** shows; the level of quality depends upon the establishment. Lovers of this type of spectacle will be delighted by the world-famous **Tropicana** in Marianao, and the Cabaret Parisien at **Hotel Nacional** In Vedado (See Landmarks).

Cabaret programs are staged by other hotels in Havana too, like the Hotel Riviera Havana's Copa Room, as well as in Varadero, such as the Varadero Internacional Hotel's Continental Cabaret.

If you prefer a more intimate and authentic environment, have a drink and dance at La Casa de la Amistad or go to a special evening of entertainment organized by the local Casa de la Cultura. Many of Havana's **restaurants** combine dining with an evening of live entertainment, like Cafe Taberna in Old Havana. Unfortunately most of the bars, clubs and other hot spots in Havana are too spread out for a pub crawl, so it's best to take a taxi (see Touring Tip). However some **bars** tend to be clustered along Old Havana's Calle Obispo, permitting some bar hopping up the pedestrianized street. Below are a variety of options, arranged by districts, for your sizzling—or subdued—nights out (see also Landmarks With A Beat):

For a listing of entertainment in the city, visit **http://habana.kewelta.cu.**

La Habana Vieja

Bar Havana Club (Map II, C3) *262 Calle San Pedro. (7) 624 108.* Enjoy a cocktail and live music at this atmospheric, dark-wood bar that is part of the **Fundación Havana Club** (see Districts).

La Bodeguita del Medio (Map III, A1) *207 Calle Empedrado, between Calles Cuba and San Ignacio. (7) 867 1374/75. Noon–midnight.* Hemingway was a regular at this iconic hangout, where he downed a mojito or two at the bar (see Hotels).

El Floridita (Map II, A3) *corner of Calle Obispo and Avenida de*

Bar Havana Club

©Claire Boobbyer/Michelin

MUST DO

Jineteros

Jinetero (or jinetera) literally means 'jockey'. The word is used to mean Cubans who ride on the back of tourists. In its milder form, it is hustling; in its most unpleasant, it is prostitution. At its most wearing, it is *jineteros* on foot or bicycle who divert you (in multiple clever ways) from a booked *casa particular (see p140)*. While many Cubans make money from tourist services, this derogatory term is applied to people who work the streets selling cigars, sex or guide services. It can also refer to people who hassle tourists merely because they want to sit down to a drink of Cuban Cristal beer.

This practice is not uncommon, and while Westerners may not be used to it and may be fearful, it can be quite a fun way to meet people. If you do go for a drink/coffee, you will need to pick up the tab. Most Cubans cannot afford to drink or eat in tourist establishments. *Jineterismo* is a way for Cubans to supplement their state salaries.

Bélgica. (7) 866 8856. Noon–midnight. Known for its cocktail bar, this luxury establishment, and its daiquiris, were favored by Hemingway *(see Hotels).*

Hotel Ambos Mundos (Map II, C3) *153 Calles Obispo and Mercaderes, near Plaza de Armas. (7) 860 9530. T*ake the elevator to the rooftop terrace for a cocktail and a fabulous view from this hotel, Hemingway's residence for some 8 years. *See Hotels.*

Café Paris (Map II, B2) *corner of Calles Obispo and San Ignacio.* Usually crowded, this Old Town bar and restaurant has long attracted tourists and locals for live music *(nightly)*, drinks and conviviality. It's a great place for people-watching and partying.

Mesón de la Flota opens at noon with a **flamenco** performance that is repeated every evening: heels tap wildly on the wood floor, castanets click, guitars are strummed with finesse, and voices are fiery. The Cuban dancers imitate the moves of Andalucian dancers. Customers can eat pretty well here. As one would expect, there is paella *(see Restaurants).*

Casa de la Música (Map IV, C2) *255 Calle Galiano, between Neptuno and Concordia. (7) 860 8296. Concerts 10pm–2am. Afternoons 4pm–6pm. 5–20CUC.* Excellent

Touring Tip

In the evening, be sure to **arrive early** enough to get a table, even if the headline act doesn't begin until after midnight. In terms of **dress code**, the more glamorous your attire, the better. Some **cover charges** include a first drink. If you meet Cubans at the door *(see sidebar on jineteros)* or take friends with you, you will be expected to pay the cover charges and the cost of drinks for them. Make sure you take enough **cash** with you. If you go to the more well-known establishments, your bar bill could be high. Many of the late-night venues are in far-flung districts, so it's best to **take a taxi.** Taxis wait outside these venues for the trip home too. Not all the buzz happens at night: matinee performances are extremely popular too.

NIGHTLIFE

125

Out and About

Finding out what's hip and happening in Havana is notoriously difficult. The most reliable source is a website run by university students: *http://habana.kewelta.cu*.

En vogue nightspots include **El Sauce** *(9th Avenida between Calles 120 and 130, Playa, 7 204 7114; www.cubarte.cult.cu/docs/sauce/sauce.pdf)*, an alfresco barn-style complex with entrance in national pesos that has been declared a reggaeton-free zone. Recent acts include Qva Libre Cuban actor Luis Alberto García who DJs, providing a musical mix with everything but reggaeton, *trovador* Frank Delgado, Buena Fé and Descemer Bueno. Another new bar, **Club Barbaram Pepito's Bar** *(Calle 26 between Avenida Zoológico and 47, Nuevo Vedado, 7 881 1808; www.cubarte.cult.cu/docs/barbaram/barbaram.pdf; closed Mon)* features designs by filmmaker Juan Padrón using characters from his *Vampires in Havana* movie. Pepito's is open to various acts such as the young *trovador* Tony Avila taking to the small stage in this intimate bar. Also look for singer-songwriters at the small theater in the **Museo de Bellas Artes** (Arte Cubano) *(7 863 9484 ext 108; www.cubarte.cult.cu/docs/mnba/mnba.pdf)*, where a roster of acts plays nightly. Recent concerts have hosted singer Danay Suarez and *trovador* Gerardo Alfonso.

ambiance in this centrally located concert hall. The biggest Cuban groups book here towards the end of the week.

El Jelengue de Areito (Map IV, C2) *410 Calle San Miguel, between Calles Campanario and Lealtad. 10pm–midnight. Live music 5pm–7pm. 20CUC.* This new Egrem-run space is an intimate joint showcasing son, trova, nueva canción cubana, bolero, salsa and rumba in the small covered yard.

Vedado

Hurón Azul (UNEAC) (Map IV, A2) *corner of 17th Avenida and Calle H.* At the home base of the National Union of Cuban writers and artists, there are concerts and other entertainment. The matinee and evening program is posted at the entrance.

Café Cantante (Map IV, A3) *corner of Paseo and 39th Avenue. (7) 879 0710. 10CUC.* Located in the basement of the Teatro

Nacional *(see Performing Arts)*, this venue invites the biggest salsa bands. It becomes a disco in the evening when there are no concerts. Proper dress required.

Habana Café (Map 1, B1) *in the Meliá Cohiba Hotel, between 1st and 3rd Paseo. (7) 33 3636. Noon–2am. Drinks minimum 10CUC.* In a 1950s setting with an airplane in the ceiling, as well as a full-size car and motorcycle in the room, this cafe presents high quality concerts (from 9pm). Be sure to make a reservation.

El Gato Tuerto (Map IV, B1) *Calle O, between Calles 17 and 19. (7) 838 2696. 11pm–4am. 10CUC with one drink.* Intimate and dim-lit, this beautiful setting, like the music you hear, is the place for excellent bolero. Since the 1960s, well-known singers have started their careers here. A magnet for couples.

La Zorra y el Cuervo (Map IV, B1), *corner Calle 23 (La Rampa) and*

MUST DO

Calle O. (7) 883 2402. 10pm–1am. 10CUC with one drink. This house of jazz pulls in fans of the genre early in the week; at the end of the week, Afro-Cuban rhythms take over *(See Landmarks).*

El Salon Rojo (Map IV, B1) *in the Capri Hotel, Avenida 21 between Calles N and O. 10pm–4am. 10CUC–35CUC with a drink.* This salon presents a sensational and quality show beginning at 11:30pm. Arrive early to get a table.

El Turquino, on the top floor at the Hotel Tryp Habana Libre *(see Hotels)*, presents a show every evening at around 10pm *(about 15CUC)* that combines cabaret, comedy and live music.

El Pico Blanco, on the top floor of the Saint John's Hotel, features disco *(Thu–Sun 9pm–3am; about 5CUC)* in a pleasant, intimate room.

Sábado de la Rumba (Map IV, off the map) *103 Calle 4, between Calle 7(Calzada) and Avenida 5 (Vedado). (7) 830 3060. 5CUC.* Shows by the Conjunto Folklórico Nacional are held Saturday afternoons at 3pm. Traditional Afro-Cuban drums and dances *(see Landmarks).*

Copa Room (Map II), *in the Habana Hotel Riviera, Paseo at Malecón. (7) 836 4051. 10pm–3am.* The Habana Hotel Riviera, around since 1957, is famous for the cabaret in its Copa Room. Wednesday nights are salsa nights, with live bands.

Miramar

La Cecilia *(see Restaurants)* presents concerts in its attractive garden from Thursday to Sunday evenings beginning at 9pm. Programs are posted at the entrance to the popular restaurant.

Casa de la Música (Map V, B1) *corner Calle 35 and Calle 20. (7) 204 0447. Concerts from 10pm – 2am. Matinees from 4pm–7pm. About 20CUC.* This institution is revered by lovers of good salsa.

Salon Rosado Tropical (Map V, B2) *corner of Avenida 41 and Calle 46. (7) 202 1467. 9pm–2am. 5CUC.* Outdoor dancing in an inviting atmosphere. Rosado gets crowded, though.

La Maison (Map V, B1) *corner Avenida 7 and Calle 16.* At La Maison, there's a piano bar daily *(3pm–9pm)*. On certain evenings *(11pm–4am)*, salsa concerts are held in the pretty garden.

Marianao

Tropicana (Map V, B2) *corner Calle 72 and Avenida 41, in Marianao. (7) 267-1718. Shows daily 10pm–2am. 70-90CUC depending on seat; with meal, from 70CUC.* Since its opening in 1939, this institution has boasted many celebrities in its audiences as well as on its huge, open-air stage *(see Landmarks).*

Varadero

Casa Blanca Bar, atop the Mansión Xanadú *(see Hotels)*, is a good spot for a quiet drink and the sounds of jazz or Cuban traditional music. Take in **views** of the coastline while sipping a cocktail in this top-floor bar.

Casa de la Música, *Avenida Playa between Calles 42 and 43. (45) 66 8918.* This venue in Varadero town attracts big-name acts. Sizzling nights kick off at 10:30pm and go until 3am. Matinees are billed from 5pm to 9pm.

RESTAURANTS

It is fair to say that most visitors to Havana won't rush back for the food. With few exceptions, Cuban food tends to be bland, monotonous and unexciting. It's understandable if you think the food lacks variety, but keep in mind that years of rationing, shortages and import restrictions have seriously limited consumer choice. It's best to be kind to the apologetic waiter who might occasionally have to turn down your request with a helpless *Se acabó* ("We run out"). What the food may lack in variety or flavor, the lovely settings of many of Havana's restaurants make up for—in abundance. Imagine dining in a tropically planted patio under the night stars to the sounds of a live band, or within a historic colonial villa, appointed with exquisite tiles or woodwork. The final ingredient to your dining experience here is the famous Cuban hospitality: expect to be welcomed with warmth, cheerfulness and even a sense of humor, especially if dining in a *paladar* (**private restaurant**). With a few exceptions, the best culinary experiences will be found in *paladares*.

Prices and Amenities

The restaurants here were selected for their ambience, location, regional dishes and/or value for money. Prices indicate the average cost of a dinner for one adult (not including beverages or service charges). In Cuba there is no sales or food tax, but some tourist restaurants add a **service charge** of 10 percent to their bills. Most restaurants are open every day, except where noted. Very few restaurants, except hotel restaurants, accept credit cards (credit cards from the US are not accepted). **Tipping** *(la propina)* is expected. It's advisable to tip at least 1CUC or more, depending on the service rendered, but avoid exorbitant tips. Check first to see if a service charge has been added to your bill. The following legend indicates the price ranges for the restaurants described.

$ <10CUC
$$ 10-20CUC
$$$ 20-50CUC
$$$$ >50CUC

Dining Venues

Casas particulares

You're renting a room in a private home, but contrary to bed and breakfast inns as we know them, your host can fix you dinner (at an extra charge). We strongly recommend that you take advantage of this opportunity. You'll be served uncomplicated, usually delicious home cooking in the comfort of a home. For 10CUC on average, you won't find a better value.

Hotels

Although most hotels have a restaurant, you'll find that the tedious mix of pork and chicken, rice and chips they serve rarely justifies the bill. In major hotels, international cuisine is generally on the menu, and some seaside resorts even offer "all-you-can-eat" buffets to their guests. Expect a minimum rate of 15-20CUC per meal. Some luxury hotels have quality restaurants that serve good international food, but at a cost of 30CUC per person on average.

Restaurants

In cities or areas of particular interest, **restaurants for tourists** are more and more common. They serve both international and Creole cuisine, and occasionally some regional specialties, for about 12CUC per person (more than twice that price if you order lobster, which is spiny lobster, not like Maine lobster). But except for a few upscale restaurants, you can't be sure of quality food on your plate. Service may well also be lackluster. Another option is to eat at a restaurant for Cubans with a menu in CUP *(see Money)*. However, do not expect a great selection of dishes there nor any kind of gourmet food.

Paladares

Paladares (meaning "palate," or "taste") were named after a restaurant in a Brazilian telenovela that was popular in Cuba back in the early 1990s—at the beginning of the "Special Period," when Cuba was plunged into an economic crisis. *Paladares* started flourishing then and have sprung up ever since. These home-based, family-run restaurants are now no longer limited to 12 tables only, and can be a delightful way to have a complete meal for 10-20CUC on average, in a welcoming atmosphere. Many *paladares* invite you straight into their private kitchen or dining room transformed to accommodate a few clients. In some cases, you will just eat authentic food on a corner of the family table, facing the television. Other *paladares* are

a lot fancier, and you may actually have a hard time telling them apart from classic **state-run restaurants** (although the gulf between service is very noticeable).

Street Food

Culinary options at the street level are rather limited. A few pesos will get you cold drinks *(refrescos)*, excellent **milkshakes** *(batidos)*, candy or poor ice cream.
If you have something more substantial in mind, all you can expect to find is the usual *pan con lechón* (a rather fat piece of pork stuffed between two slices of bread), unless you go to the nearest farmers' market to buy fruits and vegetables.
Another option is to try one of the frozen **pizzas** that locals sometimes sell on their doorstep. Since the relaxation on laws governing self-employment, more Cubans are operating street stalls, restaurants and pizzerias. Finally, if you are on the road, rather than going hungry, make a quick stop at a Servicupet gas station for biscuits and other snacks.

Street food

©Sylvaine Poitau/Apa Publications

Cuisine

Cuban cuisine is an elaborate blend of Spanish, African and Caribbean influences, the latter being the major contributor. Cuban food is rich in fat and starches, but tends to use spices sparingly due to lack of availability. Most Cuban cooking relies on just the basic spices such as garlic and pepper.

Creole Dishes

Most establishments offer Creole dishes based on **pork** *(puerco* or *cerdo)* or **chicken** *(pollo)*—grilled or fried—served with **rice** and **black beans, plantains** and **cassava** *(yucca)*. A tomato, cucumber, cabbage or avocado **salad** (depending on the season) and **boniato** chips (a kind of sweet potato) may be added to the meal. These staple foods, which form the basis of the traditional Cuban diet, can be prepared in a variety of ways. For instance, the ever-present rice *(arroz)* is served plain or *congrí* (with red beans), or as the popular **moros y cristianos** (literally "Moors and Christians," a metaphor for this mixture of white rice and black beans). Plantains come in all forms and shapes. They can be puréed *(fufú de plátano)* or fried *(plátanos fritos)*. They can also be twice-fried to produce

Lobster dinner

©Sylvaine Poitau/Apa Publications

patties *(tostones)* or finely chopped and deep-fried to produce chips *(mariquitas)*.

Desserts

One of the classic desserts consists of guava fruit served with soft white cheese or grated cheese. From May on, fruit lovers can enjoy mangoes, while wintertime brings bananas, pineapples, tangerines and sweet grapefruits (particularly those from Viñales) to the table. Mamey *(zapote)* is also a prized fruit that makes a delicious milkshake or ice cream. Other popular alternatives for dessert include *flan* (caramel-flavored custard) and bread or rice puddings. If the latter doesn't appeal to you, try a selection of Coppelia ice cream *(see Districts)*, and end your meal with a *café cubano* (strong and sweet).

Fish

Seafood and fish dishes are increasingly served in Cuba. Prior to 2011, it was illegal for *paladares* to serve lobster, shrimp and beef *(res)*. Cubans usually prepare fish with a tomato-based, heavily-salted Spanish Creole sauce *(langosta enchilada)*, but you can have it grilled, if you prefer.

Cuban Specialties

Apart from Havana, where you'll find a good number of fine-dining restaurants, **Baracoa** (located in the Guantánamo province) is known all over the country for its coconut and fish dishes. It is particularly famous for its outstanding **ajiaco** (the Cuban national dish, consisting of a meat and vegetable stew served with yucca bread), but also for local specialties such as *cururucho* (a sweet mix of coconut and various fruits wrapped in a palm leaf) and *tetí* (a fish delicacy).

Drinks

In Havana and *casas particulares*, you can enjoy fresh tropical fruit juices. Carton drinks or sodas (*refrescos*), such as Tropicola (local cola drink) or Cachito (a Cuban version of 7-Up), are cheaper than the tinned Coca-Cola (from the Mexico plant) and Sprite that are also available. Street vendors will sometimes sell banana or guava *batidos* (milkshakes) for a few pesos. In rural areas, the traditional sugarcane juice is known as *guarapo*.

Cuba produces **rum** of the finest quality. Bottles of **Havana Club**—the most popular national brand—literally flood the market. Gold rums such as Carta de Oro (5 year old) or Añejo (7 year old) can be enjoyed straight or on the rocks. Light rums Carta Blanca (3 year old) form the basis of the many **cocktails** for which Cuba is famous. Classic Cuban cocktails are the **Cuba Libre** (rum, cola, lemon juice and ice), the **mojito** (rum, lemon, sparkling water, ice and hierbabuena leaves) and the **daiquirí** (rum, lemon juice, sugar, maraschino, crushed ice). A wide variety is yours for the tasting: Ron Collins, Papa's special, Cuba bella, Cubanito, Mulata, Piña colada, punch and many more.

True oenophiles definitely won't be impressed by Cuban wine: the Soroa wine is mediocre and sweet. You'll be better off ordering **mineral water** such as Ciego Montero (the most common brand in Cuba) or **beer** (*cerveza*). Foreign brands are available, but try quality local beers such as Bucanero (the most popular brand in Havana), Cristal (which is lighter) or Mayabe.

La Habana Vieja

$ La Casa de la Parra

(Map II, A3). *Corner of Calles Brasil and Bernaza. (7) 867 1029. 11am–11pm.*
This small restaurant with a patio is located only three blocks from the Capitol. Expect on the menu a variety of traditional Creole dishes. Budget meals, music bands and an eclectic mix of customers make La Casa a friendly address. **Creole.**

$ Torre la Vega

(Map III, B2). *114 Calle Obrapla, between Calles Mercaderes and Oficios. (7) 860 6524. 10am–9pm.*
This cafeteria-type eatery serves decent, inexpensive Creole meals on a pleasant terrace overlooking the tree-shaded plaza on the other side of a pedestrian street. The variety of dishes is limited, but fresh fruit juices and *batidos* make up for it. **Creole.**

$$ La Bodeguita del Medio

(Map III, A1). *207 Calle Empedrado, between Calles Cuba and San Ignacio. (7) 867 1375. Noon–midnight.*
Just a short walk from the cathedral, this iconic hangout dates to the 1940s. Hemingway would regularly come here for mojitos. The walls are covered with photos, graffiti and signatures of celebrities and ordinary patrons alike. Good Creole cuisine and cocktails are the restaurant's trademark. Enjoy a mojito at the bar, in the indoor dining area

downstairs or on the terrace on the upper level. Reservations recommended. **Creole.**

🍴 $$ La Imprenta

(Map II, C2). *Calle Mercaderes, between Calles Lamparilla and Amargura. (7) 864 9851. Noon–11pm.*

This attractive state-run restaurant sits inside a former printworks. Dine on light dishes of meats and fish in this well-run eatery in the heart of the Old Town. The service and the quality and variety of food are noteworthy. **Creole.**

$$ Al Medina

(Map III, B2). *12 Calle Oficios, between Calles Obispo and Obrapía. (7) 867 1041. www.habaguanex.cu. Noon–midnight.*

Housed in a fine 17C Colonial-style mansion with a patio, this restaurant offers a Middle-Eastern alternative to fried or grilled chicken. *Mezze,* falafel, hummus and mutton dishes are served on large copper plates. **Middle-Eastern**.

🍴 $$ El Mesón de la Flota

(Map II, C3). *257 Calle Mercaderes, between Calles Amargura and Brasil. (7) 863 3838. www.haba guanex.cu. Noon–11pm.*

For a taste of Spanish culture, look no farther than this atmospheric restaurant, where you'll get to watch flamenco dancers and musicians perform while enjoying paella and tapas. **Spanish.**

$$ La Moneda

(Map III, A2). *77 Calle San Ignacio, between Plaza de la Catedral and O'Reilly. (7) 867 3852. Noon–midnight.*

Set in a prime location near the cathedral, this hole-in-the-wall space is a friendly place to eat. It offers classic Cuban dishes such as pork, chicken, fish or omelets with black bean rice, fried plantain and salad. Its walls are decorated with coins and banknotes from all over the world. **Creole.**

🍴 $$ La Mulata del Sabor

(Map II, C3). *153 Calle Sol, corner of Calle San Ignacio. (7) 867 5984. 12:30pm–11pm. Closed Sun.*

This little *paladar* is very popular among locals, a sure sign that it is a good pick. At lunchtime, you'll see them carry out the daily special (3CUC). But most action occurs in the evening. Justina, the colorful owner, knows how to draw crowds with her decent Creole cuisine and great personality. **Creole.**

$$ La Taberna de la Muralla

(Map II, C3). *Plaza Vieja, corner of CallesSan Ignacio and Muralla. (7) 866 4453. 11am–midnight.*

You'll love this brewpub with its gleaming alembics (distillation apparatus) and own beer brewed in-house. The grills and kebabs served on the terrace are definitely worth trying. **International.**

$$$ La Barca

(Map III, B2). *Corner of Avenida del Puerto and Calle Obispo. (7) 866 8807. www.habaguanex.cu. Noon–midnight.*

This restaurant opened its doors in 2008. Having such a gifted neighbor as El Templete could have been a real challenge for any newcomer, but talent does not depend upon age, and La Barca is living proof of it. Hidden behind the arcades of its façade, the open-air dining area serves Creole dishes that include a grilled piglet special for 4 to 6 people. **Creole/International.**

$$$ Café del Oriente
(Map II, C3). *112 Calle Oficios. Plaza San Francisco. (7) 860 6686. www.habaguanex.cu. Noon–midnight.*
If you prefer International cuisine, you should try this establishment. You'll be attracted by its smart interior from olden days and by its pleasant terrace. **International.**

$$$ El Floridita
(Map II, A3). *557 Calle Obispo and Calle Monserrate. (7) 867 1299. www.floridita-cuba.com. 11am–midnight.*

El Floridita

©Sylvaine Poitau/Apa Publications

Best known for its cocktail bar, this luxury establishment was one of Hemingway's favorite haunts in Havana. Tuxedo-clad waiters offer fish and seafood specialties at outrageous rates. **Seafood.**

$$$ El Patio
(Map III, A1). *Plaza de la Catedral, corner of Calle San Ignacio. (7) 867 1034. www.habaguanex.cu. Noon–midnight.*
An 18C mansion called Casa del Marqués de Aguas Claras is home to this restaurant, whose setting alone justifies the bill, although the service doesn't quite follow suit. Creole and seafood dishes are served to the sounds of live music in the inner courtyard, on the balcony, or on the outdoor patio facing the cathedral. **Creole/International**

$$$ El Templete
(Map III, B1). *Corner of Avenida del Puerto and Calle Narciso López. (7) 866 8807. www.habaguanex.cu. Noon–midnight.*
Opened in 2004, this upscale establishment has quickly become one of the top-listed restaurants in Havana. The marine theme, brought out by the blue hues of its interior, is befitting of the seafood dishes and other fancy concoctions prepared by expert hands and served on starched tablecloths. **Seafood.**

$$$ Roof Garden Torredel Oro
Top floor of the Mercure Sevilla Hotel, 55 Trocadero, between Calle Zulueta and Prado. (7) 860 8560. www.accorhotels.com. 7pm–9:30pm.
Now transformed into a dining space, this former ballroom from the early 20C affords exceptional views of Havana. Here, the cuisine and service definitely live up to the wonderful setting and decor, complete with high-coffered ceilings. **French.**

RESTAURANTS

A Trio of Cafes in La Habana Vieja

Café O'Reilly, *203 Calle O'Reilly at San Ignacio*. This Old Town mainstay is perfectly situated close to the cathedral. The wrought-iron spiral staircase leads to a second floor with a small veranda overlooking the street.

Café Lamparilla, *54 Calle Lamparilla, between Mercaderes and San Ignacio*. Tables and chairs under white awnings in the heart of the Old Town provide a perfect break in this pedestrianized street. There's a nice view of the Stock Exchange. Tapas available.

Café Escorial, *Mercaderes at Muralla*. This cafe is the loveliest one in La Habana Vieja. Enjoy liqueur coffees and croissants served under white canvas umbrellas overlooking the Plaza Vieja. The aroma of coffee adds to the ambience. Good ice cream, too.

Centro Habana

$$ Asahi

(Map IV, C2). *364 Calle Lealtad, between Calles San Rafael and San Miguel. (7) 878 7194. 11am–11pm.* This *paladar* may be a bit impersonal, but its cooks prepare fine fish dishes that are nicely complemented by *tostones* (fried plantain chips) and sides of savory rice. **Creole/Seafood.**

$$ Castropol

(Map IV, C1). *107 Malecon, between Calles Genios and Crespo. (7) 861 4867. Noon–midnight.* A rare set-up in Cuba, this cooperative society restaurant has an excellent location with ocean views. It serves a wide variety of seafood dishes on its first-floor al fresco terrace and icily air-conditioned dining room. Downstairs on the ground floor, diners enjoy grilled foods. **Seafood.**

$$ San Cristobal

(Map IV, C2). *469 Calle San Rafael, between Calles Lealtad and Campanario. (05) 292 1305. Noon–midnight. Closed Sun.*

San Cristobal

©Claire Boobbyer/Michelin

This beautiful house is decorated with old photos, antiques, curios, objets d'art and religious statues. Each room has been artfully designed by owner Carlos Cristobal. The extensive menu focuses on seafood and meat dishes Cuban style. French, Spanish and Chilean wines are available. Reservations advised at night. **Creole/Seafood.**

$$$ La Guarida

(Map IV, C2). *418 Calle Concordía, between Calles Gervasio and Escobar. (7) 866 9047. www.laguarida.com. Noon–4pm, 7pm–2am.*

This eclectic-looking *paladar* has become a trendy place ever since it was used as a setting for the Cuban-Spanish-Mexican co-produced film *Strawberry and Chocolate*. It now proudly exhibits photos of its illustrious clients. The cuisine is elaborate, and its inventiveness is definitely disguised from other establishments. Sugarcane, honey, lemon, coconut, mango and other tropical fruits—all culinary riches of the island—are used to spice up the menu and largely make up for short supplies. Prices are understandably high. Reservations recommended. **Creole.**

Vedado

$ Monguito
(Map IV, B2). *408 Calle L, between Calles 23 and 25. (7) 831 2615. Noon–11pm. Closed Thu.*
Sitting right across the Habana Libre Hotel, this tiny *paladar* is sure to enchant you with its generous, inexpensive Creole cooking and its kitchy atmosphere. **Creole.**

$ Nerei
(Map IV, B1). *110 Calle 19, corner of Calle L. (7) 832 7860. Noon–midnight.*
Located in the vicinity of several great hotels, this *paladar* is housed in an old, airy house graced with a beautiful terrace. The menu boasts invigorating Creole dishes, and occasionally some good seafood as well. **Creole.**

$$ Atelier
(Map IV, A1, off map), *511 Calle 5, between Calle 2 and Paseo. (7) 836 2025. atelierde5ta@yahoo.es. Call for reservations. Noon–midnight.*

A white-washed mansion has been converted into an artfully decorated dining room with two adjoining roof terraces. Starters of asparagus au gratin and baba ganoush can be hit and miss, but reliable choices include the filet mignon and the fish with roast garlic. Both are accompanied by a tasty ratatouille and rice. **Creole.**

$$ Los Amigos
(Map IV, B1). *253 Calle M, between Calles 19 and 21. (7) 830 0880. Noon–midnight.*
Good Creole cuisine here draws an essentially Cuban crowd. The restaurant's stellar reputation has spread around the neighborhood, so be ready to stand in line. **Creole.**

$$ Café Laurent
(Map IV, B1). *Penthouse, 257 Calle M, between Calles 19 and 21. (7) 832 6890. Noon–midnight.*
Ride the 1950s elevator to the penthouse suite converted into one of the newest paladars in town. A modern, fresh feel with a wonderful terrace is offset by some handsome 1950s furniture. Dine on perfectly cooked tuna, huge portions of lamb, grilled shrimp and octopus. Service is excellent. **International.**

$$ La Casona de 17
(Map IV, B1). *60 Avenida 17, between Calles M and N. (7) 838 3136. Noon–2am.*
In this little restaurant, set in a mansion opposite the Edificio Focsa, the traditional Cuban dishes are a bit pricey. For a more affordable meal, check out the chicken dishes and pizzas served cafeteria-style on the terrace. **Creole/International.**

$$ La Rampa

Ground floor of the TRYP Habana Libre Hotel, Calle L between Calles 23 and 25. (7) 834 6158. www.solmeliacuba.com. Open 24hrs daily.

This air-conditioned cafeteria offers a great choice of decent International dishes, such as steaks, pasta and, above all, mixed salads—a nice alternative to fried chicken. **International.**

$$ Unión Francesa de Cuba

(Map IV, A2). *Avenida 17 and Calle 6. (7) 832 4493. Noon–midnight.*

Despite its name and old photographs of Paris, this eatery is an all-Cuban restaurant. Several types of meals are yours for the choosing; the value is hard to beat. For a moderately-priced meal, try the grills on the terrace of the upper level, or check out the 2nd floor for its selection of pizzas and pastas, and very affordable full-course menus. A more refined, more expensive cuisine is offered in a secluded restaurant room on the ground floor. **Creole/Italian.**

$$$ El Gringo Viejo

(Map IV, A2). *454 Calle 21, between Calles E and F. (7) 831 1946. Noon–11pm.*

Beside traditional Creole cuisine, you may be fortunate enough to enjoy a succulent crab or some other seafood dish. Note that the service is fast (perhaps too fast) and that both air-conditioned dining rooms are non-smoking only. **Creole/International.**

$$$ Restaurante 1830

(Map V, B1). *1252 Malecón, corner of Calle 20. (7) 838 3090. Noon–midnight.*

This stylish restaurant is particularly renowned for its Japanese island garden, where the Almendares River meets the Ocean. Bridges, terraces and fountains make it a lovely place to stroll, dance or attend a concert. The restaurant itself offers decent seafood and International cuisine. **Creole/International.**

Nuevo Vedado

Sushi night, Restaurante La Casa

©Claire Boobbyer/Michelin

$$ Restaurante La Casa

(Map IV, A3, off map). *865 Calle 30, between Calles 26 and 41. (7) 881 7000. http://restaurantelacasacuba.com. Noon–midnight.*

This family-run business in a fashionable 1950s house serves a smorgasbord of fish, chicken and rabbit. Dine alfresco among waterfalls and fairy lights and try the Pica Pica La Casa, a mixed tasting option. The coconut ice cream served in a half nut is sublime. Service is friendly and attentive. **Creole/International.**

Miramar and Playa

$ El Palenque
(Map V, A2). *Avenida 17 and Calle 190 (Siboney), Playa. (7) 203 8222. Noon–midnight.*
This large open-air, U-shaped restaurant is state run. Delicious Italian food (pizza corner) and Creole cuisine are the mainstays. Customers enjoy tender meat and generous portions at reasonable prices. **Italian/Creole.**

$$ El Aljibe
(Map V, B1). *Avenida 7, between Calles 24 and 26. (7) 203 1583. Noon–midnight.*
This informal restaurant is famous for its chicken-based recipes, including the house special *pollo criollo*, served with rice, salad, potatoes and "all-you-can-eat" fried plantain. A good wine list and copious meals served by an efficient staff are the restaurant's hallmarks. Good value for the money. **Creole.**

$$ La Cecilia
(Map V, A2). *11010 Avenida 5, between Calles 110 and 112, Playa. (7) 204 1562. Noon–midnight.*
La Cecilia specializes in Creole and International cuisine, grilled meat and fried fish. All rooms open onto a lush garden with tropical plants, so take a jacket or a sweater with you if you plan to eat here on a cool winter evening.
There is a small cabaret with the dinner service for those willing to dance the salsa to the sound of a live orchestra. **Creole/International.**

$$ Doctor Café
(Map V, B1). *111 Calle 28, between Calles 1 and 3. (7) 203 4718. Noon–midnight.*
This small, family-run restaurant is located on a quiet street neighboring the Malecón, a world away from the city's bustle. You can dine in the cozy dining room or on the lovely, secluded patio. Relax and enjoy the delicious rabbit *(conejo)* specialty, cooked in garlic or beer. **Creole.**

$$ El Palio
(Map V, B1). *Avenida 1, between Calles 24 and 26. (7) 202 9869. Noon–midnight.*
Hidden behind high walls, just a block from the ocean, this *paladar* features Creole cuisine with a flair, including *vaca frita di Camagüey* (flank steak), served by a friendly staff. You may find the drafts of freezing air from the air-conditioning a bit unpleasant, so bring a sweater with you, just in case. **Italian/Creole.**

$$$ La Cocina de Lilliam
(Map V, B1). *1311 Calle 48, between Calles 13 and 15. (7) 209 6514. www.lacocinadelilliam.com. Noon–midnight.*
Former US President Jimmy Carter ate in this *paladar* back in 2002, which is a great source of pride for the owner. Visitors will be served their meals in a sumptuous mansion, complete with a lush patio echoing the sound of gurgling fountains. One of the specialties of the house is the *ropa vieja*, a delicious mutton stew. It is advisable to reserve a table in advance. **Creole/International.**

RESTAURANTS

$$$ La Ferminia

(Map V, A2). *18207 Avenida 5, between Calles 182 and 184, Playa. (7) 204 6555. Noon–midnight.*
The former apartments of this elegant mansion were converted into private lounges. Rare woodwork, embroidered tablecloths and exotic plants add to the stylish decor. Enjoy wood-grilled meat or fish, among other delicacies. **International.**

$$$ La Paila

(Map V, B2). *Corner of Calle 88-B and Calle 51-A (Marianao). (7) 267 0282. Noon–11pm. Reservations only.*
This *paladar* is really off the beaten track. Otherwise, everything is perfect about it, from the soft-lit lanterns of its romantic terrace garden to its delicious cuisine. The talented chef, who practiced his art in one Havana's major hotels, now delights diners with his inspired dishes, such as the excellent tuna in pastry. Friendly staff. **Creole.**

$$$ El Tocororo

(Map V, B1). *302 Calle 18, corner of Avenida 3. (7) 202 4530. 12:30pm–midnight. Closed Sun.*
One of the capital's finest establishments, this government-run restaurant is particularly popular with foreign diplomats. Housed in an old mansion, it features richly decorated lounges, stained glass, Tiffany lamps and artificial Cuban trogons or *tocororos* (the national bird) hidden amid exotic plants. Spiny lobster and other seafood specialties are on the menu, which definitely measures up to the setting. **Seafood.**

El Tocororo

©Claire Boobbyer/Michelin

Playas del Este

Hotels in Playas del Este are all-inclusive (meals are included in the rate). Beachside shacks are also available to provide a quick meal.

$ Mi Cayito

Laguna Itabo, Santa María del Mar. (4) 797 1339. 10am–6pm.
Located next to Hotel Blau Arenal, between the lagoon and the beach, this busy bar and restaurant serves up shrimp, fish and crawfish in an open-air setting. **Seafood.**

$ Piccolo Paladar

Avenida 5, between Calles 502 and 504, Guanabo. (4) 796 4300. 11am–11pm.
Local products (some raised on-site) come to the fore at this excellent eatery. Opt for dishes featuring vegetables or locally raised pork, rather than pasta or pizza. **Italian.**

$$ Pizzeria Don Peppo

503 Calle 482, between Avenidas 5 and 7, Guanabo. www.cubana sol.com/pallandar/donpeppo.htm. 11am–10pm.
This welcoming eatery is run by a jovial Italian and offers excellent wood-fired pizzas as well as fish at decent prices. **Italian.**

Varadero

$ Castel Nuovo
(Map I, A2). *503 Avenida 1 and Calle 11. (45) 66 7786. Noon–11pm.*
Located at the outskirts of the town, this Italian eatery concocts a good selection of well-prepared specialties like pasta and pizza. The decor is less casual than other beach spots, and the prices are right. **Italian.**

$ Ranchón El Compay
(Map I, E1). *Corner of Avenida Playa and Calle 54. (45) 61 2460. 10:30am–10pm.*
At this pleasant spot with a palm-thatched roof you can order up steak or chicken with fries and gaze at the ocean blue. **Creole.**

$ La Vega
(Map I, C1). *Corner of Avenida Playa and Calle 31. (45) 61 1430. Noon–9pm.*
Behind the cigar shop and the La Bodegona grocery store, a few tables sit on a pretty wood terrace facing the water. At this eatery, you'll find tasty fish dishes, and savory items from the grill. Service is good, and unlike many spots in Varadero, there's no reggaeton music blasting from the sound system. **Creole.**

$$ El Bodegón Criollo
(Map I, D1). *Corner of Avenida Playa and Calle 40. (45) 66 7784. Noon–11pm.*
This restaurant replicates Havana's La Bodeguita del Medio, with its graffiti-covered walls and red-beamed ceilings. Have dinner or just a drink on the pleasant terrace only steps from the beach. The kitchen serves a variety of tasty Creole dishes at fair prices. **Creole.**

$$ La Casa del Chef
(Map I, A-B1). *Avenida1, between Calles 12 and 13. (45) 61 3606. 2:30pm–10pm.*
This spot is ideal for people-watching. A complete menu is offered (bean soup, choice of fish or meat, salad and dessert). The service is good, and there's often live music. **Creole/International.**

$$ El Mesón del Quijote
(Map III). *Carretera de las Américas 1KM, Reparto de la Torre. (45) 661 3522. Noon–midnight.*
A statue of Don Quixote on horseback marks the entrance to this tavern located on a hill across from the Villa Cuba hotel. Spanish dishes (try the paella) and spiny lobster entrées are served in the candlelit dining room. **Spanish.**

$$ Retiro Josone
(Map I, E2). *Avenida 1, between Calles 56 and 59.*
Three restaurants are located around Varadero's city park: **La Campana** *($; 45 66 7228; noon–11pm)* specializes in Creole cuisine in a more rustic atmosphere; **Dante** *($$; 45 66 7738; 12:30pm–3pm, 7pm–midnight, closed Sun), offers good (if somewhat pricey)* Italian dishes; and **El Retiro** *($$; 45 66 7316; noon–11pm)* offers meat, fish and other International courses at reasonable prices.

$$$$ El Restaurante Xanadú
Mansión Du Pont de Nemours. (45) 66 3850. www.varaderogolf club.com. Noon–10:30pm.
Xanadú hotel's luxurious dining room has a terrace overlooking the sea, carefully prepared French entrées and an excellent wine list. **French.**

HOTELS

Havana has a fairly broad range of accommodations for all budgets and comfort levels. Luxury hotels can be found throughout the city, but mainly in Old Havana, Vedado, Miramar and Varadero. Luxury is a relative term in Cuba; it's best not to expect world-class standards for the majority of hotels in Havana. Most hotels in Old Havana occupy grand, renovated colonial buildings. Two of Old Havana's convents even offer rooms for overnight stays, at reasonable prices. A number of historic hotels are situated around Parque Central, including Havana's oldest hotel. Larger, more modern hotels are clustered in Vedado and Miramar. Lower-priced lodgings are plentiful throughout the city in the form of *casas particulares (see below)*.

Prices and Amenities

In addition to hotels, you can also rent a **room in a private home** *(casas particulares)*, an appealing option when the home in question is a lovely Colonial-style mansion in Vedado or Old Havana. The hotels and in-home accommodations described here are classified according to the price for a **double room** for one night in high season. Since these prices may vary throughout the year, you are advised to inquire in advance and check rates during the period chosen for your stay. Nightly hotel rates usually include breakfast. Most of Havana's *casas particulares* charge about 25-30CUC/night. Plan on paying an added 3-5CUCs for breakfast in a private home. Many hotels accept **credit cards** (none accept US credit cards), but the *casas particulares* do not. All hotels and most *casas particulares* offer air conditioning, and most hotels have Internet access; only a handful of the top-end hotels provide Wi-Fi. Other than for the hotels, AC means the property is air-conditioned. Expect the major hotels to have English-speaking staff, but otherwise, Spanish predominates. All hotels have a car-rental desk, currency exchange and medical services on-site. Many of the hotels in this guide also have on-site **restaurants**. In the *casas particulares*, dinner can be arranged in advance, so inquire. *The following legend indicates the price ranges for the lodgings described:*

$ <50CUC
$$ 50CUC-75CUC
$$$ 75CUC-100CC
$$$$ 100CUC-200CUC
$$$$$ >200CUC

Reservations

If visiting Cuba in **high season** (Nov-Jan and Jul-Aug), make hotel and car reservations ahead of time, by phone, fax or email in English (if in Spanish, you might avoid misunderstandings and disappointment). With some of the major hotels, reservations can be made **online** *(see opposite)*, but be sure to get confirmation of your reservation from the hotel in writing. Some travel operators can also help you design tailor-made vacations and handle reservations for you *(see Practical Information)*. In **low season**, book your rooms in advance as well to avoid rack rate charges.

Online Booking

The official tourism website for Cuba, www.infotur.cu, lists hotels by city and gives the hotel's individual website. A growing number of hotels can be booked online, especially hotels operated by these Cuban organizations:

Cubanacán: *www.hoteles cubanacan.com*

Gaviota: *www.gaviota-grupo.com*

Gran Caribe: *www.gran-caribe.com*

Habaguanex: *www.habaguanex.cu*

Hoteles Islazul: *www.islazul.cu*

The following are recommended for reservations also:

www.cubahotelreservation.com
www.cubacasas.net
www.cuba-junky.com/cuba/cuba-casa-particulares.htm

LA HABANA VIEJA

Private Homes

Casa Colonial Azul

$ 2 rooms

(Map II, C4). *654 Calle San Ignacio, between Calles Merced and Jesús María. (7) 863 1279. pablo@ed. patrimonio.ohc.cu. AC. Private Bathroom. TV. Breakfast 4CUC.* Behind the blue and white Colonial façade is a comfortable apartment similar in style to Eugenio y Fabio, but with a private bathroom for each bedroom. A lovely homemade bar can be found on the roof terrace. Excellent staff.

Casa Dos Hermanas Yonaika y Yonaisis

$ 2 rooms

(Map II, B3). *364 Calle Luz, between Calles Aguacate and Compostela. (7) 861 1378. jesusmaria2003@ yahoo.com. AC. Private Bathroom. TV room. Breakfast 3CUC.*

The proprietors, daughters of Jesús and María *(below)*, welcome you to their large, renovated apartment on the second floor of a 1935 house. Rooms are arrayed off the spacious interior corridor. A pleasant balcony partially overlooks the Bélen Convent.

Casa Humberto

$ 2 rooms

(Map II, B3). *3rd Floor, 611 Calle Compostela, between Calles Sol and Luz. (7) 860 3264. Johnyterroni@yahoo.es. www.casahumberto.com. AC. Private Bathroom. Breakfast 5CUC.* Guests at this impeccably clean establishment can order a meal or a mojito at any hour; work out on exercise machines on the rooftop terrace; or burn a CD of their photos on the in-house computer. A night watchman opens the door for late-returning guests so that the doorbell won't wake you.

Casa Maritza Mirabal y Ramón

$ 2 rooms

(Map II, C3). *115 Calle Luz, between Calles San Ignacio and Inquisidor. (7) 862 3303. casamaritza@hotmail.com. AC. Shared Bathroom. TV. Breakfast 5CUC.* Guests are treated like royalty at this peaceful spot. The building with a blue façade features a spacious, high-ceilinged Colonial-era salon. Guest rooms open onto a nicely appointed patio. Two bedrooms share two bathrooms.

HOTELS

🛏 Eugenio y Fabio

$ **3 rooms**

(Map II, C4). *656 Calle San Ignacio, between Calles Jesús María and Merced. (7) 862 9877. fabio. quintana@infomed.sld.cu. AC. Private Bathroom. Breakfast 5CUC.*

In a handsome building with a green façade, this elaborately decorated apartment boats a Colonial-era salon overflowing with lamps, statuettes, glasware and period colonial furniture. Comfortable bedrooms are outfitted with colonial furniture. The rooftop terrace is enormous.

🛏 Jesús y María

$ **3 rooms**

(Map II, B3). *518 Calle Aguacate, between Calles Sol and Muralla. (7) 861 1378. jesusmaria2003@ yahoo.com. AC. Private Bathroom. Breakfast 5-10CUC.*

Ground-floor rooms surround a pleasant patio, but those opening onto the superb terrace with wrought-iron furniture are even nicer. The green wooden house on the top terrace is in great demand. Reservations are essential.

Nancy Pérez

$ **2 rooms.**

(Map II, B3). *207 Teniente Rey (Brasil), between Calles Habana and Aguiar. (7) 860 1898. http://casaparticularnancy perez.com. AC. Private Bathroom. Breakfast 5CUC.*

A short stairway leads to pleasant, airy rooms decorated in modern style and situated at the rear of the house, away from traffic noise. A balcony has seating overlooking the street. It's a clean and comfortable place to stay, with charming hosts.

Olga López Hernández

$ **2 rooms**

(Map II, C3). *611 Calle Cuba, between Calles Luz and Santa Clara. (7) 867 4561. olgarene50@ hotmail.com. AC. Shared Bathroom. Breakfast 3CUC (included with room in low season).*

This nicely kept apartment features pleasant patios and a salon in a handsome Colonial-style building opposite the Santa Clara convent. Often full, so reserve in advance.

Hotels

Residencia Académica Convento de Santa Clara

$ **8 rooms (30 beds).**

(Map II, C3). *610 Calle Cuba, between Calles Sol and Luz. (7) 861 3335. www.cencrem.co.cu. Fan. Shared bathrooms (private bath-room available with suite). TV room. Breakfast included. Cafe.*

This charming hostel within the Santa Clara Convent is one of the most peaceful places in Old Havana. Spacious rooms sleep 1 to 5 people, and there's a suite with a terrace at the center of the cloister.

Convento de Santa Brígida y Madre Isabel

$$$ **15 rooms**

(Map II, C3). *204 Calle Oficios, between Calles Teniente Rey and Muralla. (7) 866 4315. www.brigidine.org. AC. TV. Breakfast included.*

The resident nuns here have transformed part of their convent, located next to the church of St. Francis of Assisi, into a very well maintained hotel. Spacious, nicely appointed rooms offer a respite in the heart of Old Havana.

Hotel Plaza

$$$ **188 rooms**

(Map II, A2). *267 Ignacio Agramonte on the corner with Calle Neptuno. (7) 860 8583. www.gran-caribe.com. TV. Breakfast included. Restaurant.*
Overlooking a corner of the Parque Central, this early 20C palace was entirely renovated in 1991. Fountains adorn the entrance hall, but the guest quarters are simpler. Rooms overlook the street or an interior patio.

Ambos Mundos

$$$$ **51 rooms**

(Map III, A-B2). *153 Calle Obispo at Calle Mercaderes. (7) 860 9530. www.habaguanex.cu. TV. Breakfast included. Restaurant.*
American author Ernest Hemingway lived at this hotel, near the Plaza de Armas. His room (no. 511) has been preserved as a museum. Pleasant guest rooms are furnished in the style of the 1930s. Take the antique elevator to the rooftop terrace for a cocktail and a fabulous view.

Beltrán de Santa Cruz

$$$$ **11 rooms**

(Map II, C3). *411 Calle San Ignacio, between Calles Muralla and Sol. (7) 860 8330. www.habaguanex.cu. TV. Breakfast included.*
Near the Plaza Vieja, this hotel occupies a renovated former home of Spanish nobility, with Colonial-style furnishings. Ask for one of the rooms overlooking the verdant patio. Attentive service.

Conde de Villanueva

$$$$ **9 rooms**

(Map II, C2). *202 Calle Mercaderes on the corner of Calle Lamparilla. (7) 862 9293. www.habaguanex.cu. TV. Breakfast included. Restaurant.*

Cigar aficionados will enjoy a stay at this dignified hotel, with its comfortable, privileged atmosphere and warm decor accented with earthen tones. There's a small smoking lounge on the mezzanine. Spacious guest rooms bear the names of famous brands of Havana cigars.

Hostal Valencia

$$$$ **10 rooms**

(Map II, C2). *53 Calle Oficios, corner of Calle Obrapía. (7) 867 1037. www.habaguanex.cu. Breakfast included. Restaurant.*
Located a few yards off the Plaza de San Francisco, this pension occupies a handsome 18C Colonial mansion. Large, nicely decorated rooms open onto a shaded tiled patio. The in-house restaurant, **La Paella,** specializes in paella.

Hotel Florida

$$$$ **25 rooms**

(Map III, A2). *Corner of Calles Obispo and Cuba. (7) 862 4127. www.habaguanex.cu. TV. Breakfast included. Restaurant.*
Comfort and quality of service are hallmarks of this superbly restored palace (1885) ideally located in the heart of Old Havana. Elegant guest rooms overlook a handsome Neoclassical patio. The restaurant ranks among the finest in the city.

Hotel Inglaterra

$$$$ **83 rooms**

(Map II, A3). *416 Paseo del Prado, between Calles San Rafael and San Miguel. (7) 860 8596. www.gran-caribe.com. TV. Breakfast included. Restaurant.*
This 19C edifice is a registered National Monument. Sevillana ceramic pieces as well as palm

Hotel Inglaterra

©Claire Boobbyer/Michelin

trees grace the dining room. A pleasant bar sits on the top-floor terrace. Guest rooms overlook the quiet patio or the noisier Parque Central (some have balconies). Service can be inconsistent, and the atmosphere is a bit staid.

Hotel Parque Central
$$$$ **427 rooms**
(Map II, A2). *Calle Neptuno, between Prado and Calle Zulueta. (7) 860 6627. www.iberostar.com. TV. Breakfast included. Restaurant. Swimming Pool.*
Located across from the Parque Central, this modern hotel features comfortable rooms and modern conveniences that make it a destination for business travelers. The bar and swimming pool offer views of the city. **El Paseo** restaurant serves a wide selection of meats. The adjoining **El Torre** is the newest hotel in Havana with sleek rooms and a rooftop pool.

Hotel Tejadillo
$$$$ **32 rooms**
(Map III, A1). *12 Calle Tejadillo at Calle San Ignacio. (7) 863 7283. www.habaguanex.cu. TV. Breakfast included. Restaurant.*
This attractive hotel with yellow walls benefits from an excellent

location near the cathedral but far enough away from the crowds to guarantee a quiet atmosphere. Service is attentive, and there's a bar on the patio. Ask for a room with windows.

Mercure Sevilla
$$$$ **178 rooms**
(Map II, A2). *55 Calle Trocadero, between Calle Zulueta and Prado. (7) 860 8560. www.accorhotels.com. TV. Breakfast included. 2 restaurants. Swimming Pool.*
This Moorish-style structure *(see Cuban Classics)* is graced with lovely ceramics and a beautiful patio, but the quality of the rooms and the service is somewhat below the standard indicated by the price. There's a panoramic view of Havana from the top-floor restaurant, and guests can enjoy cocktails on the patio.

Palacio O'Farrill
$$$$ **38 rooms**
(Map II, B2). *102-108 Calle Cuba, between Calles Chacón and Tejadillo. (7) 860 5080. www.habaguanex.cu. TV. Breakfast included. Restaurant.*
Rooms at this elegant Neoclassical palace are arranged on three levels around a magnificent patio. Some rooms have balconies overlooking the street.

⚓ Hotel Santa Isabel
$$$$$ **27 rooms**
(Map III, B2). *9 Calle Baratillo, between Calles Obispo and Narciso Lopez. (7) 860 8201. www.habaguanex.cu. TV. Breakfast included. Restaurant.*
One of the loveliest (and most expensive) hotels in Havana, the Santa Isabel is ideally located on

MUST STAY

the Plaza de Armas, close to the main colonial sights. Formerly a sumptuous 18C palace, the hotel offers unequalled luxury. The number of rooms is relatively few, so be sure to reserve well in advance.

Hotel Saratoga
$$$$$ **96 rooms**
(Map II, A3). *603 Paseo del Prado at the corner of Call Dragones. (7) 868 1000. www.hotel-saratoga.com. TV. Breakfast included. 2 restaurants. Swimming Pool.*
At Havana's most luxurious address, you can relax in the rooftop pool while drinking in the view of the nearby Capitolio. Each of the spacious suites are decorated in a different theme. Enjoy an excellent breakfast at the on-site **Anacaona Restaurant**, as well as the service.

⚓ Palacio del Marqués de San Felipe y Santiago de Bejucal
$$$$$ **27 rooms**
Calle Oficios, at the corner of Calle Amargura, Plaza de San Francisco, (7) 864 9191 www.habaguanex.cu. TV. Breakfast included. Restaurant.
This grand and lofty, medium-sized hotel facing the Plaza de San Francisco is the newest addition to the Habaguanex hotel club. Rooms are modern in style and communal areas pay homage to contemporary artists, with Cuban art adorning the walls. Note the playful reception wall clock by Luis Alberto Rodríguez and the enchanting photo and paper mixed media pieces by José Manuel Fors Durán.

CENTRO HABANA

Private Homes

Casa 1932
$ **2 rooms**
Calle Campanario 62 (bajos), between Calles San Lázaro and Lagunas. (7) 863 6203. www.casahabana.net. AC. Private Bathrooms.
A casa particular with a difference, Casa 1932 is located near the Deauville Hotel. The handsome front room is decked out in antiques, Art Nouveau objet d'art and curios. Host Luis is one of the most hospitable casa owners in Cuba. His bedrooms are nicely furnished with antique heirlooms.

Hotels

BelleVue Deauville
$$ **144 rooms**
(Map IV, C1). *1 Avenida de Italia (Galiuno) and Malecón. (7) 866 8812. www.hotetur.com. TV. Breakfast included. Full board available. Restaurant. Swimming Pool.*
This 14-story tower on the busy Malecón between Old Havana and Vedado offers nicely furnished and renovated rooms with balconies and views of the coast. Ask for an upper-floor room to get away from the traffic noise. The 7th floor swimming pool boasts city views.

VEDADO

Private Homes
This expansive district has innumerable opportunities for accommodations in *casas particulares,* most of which are in superb colonial-era mansions.

HOTELS

Alejandro Martínez
$ **2 rooms**
(Map IV, A2). *655 Calle 8, between Calles 27 and Calzada de Zapata. (7) 830 9081 or 264 8029. AC.*
Guests are made to feel at home everywhere here; the house offers two bedrooms, a bathroom, kitchen, salon, and large terrace overlooking frangipani and fruit trees.

Amparo López
$ **2 rooms**
(Map IV, B1). *Apt. 2, 53 Calle Línea, between Calles M and N. (7) 832 7003. AC. Shared Bathroom.*
The two bedrooms share a bathroom in this large apartment in a modern building near the Malecón. The beds are enormous and the decor, though pleasant, is fairly somber with little natural light to enliven it. The owner, a former university professor, is friendly, offering a counterbalance to the housekeeper's cooler demeanor.

Armando y Betty Gutiérrez
$ **2 rooms**
(Map IV, B1). *62 Avenida 21, between Calles M and N. (7) 832 1876. AC.*
This large apartment, located near La Rampa and the Hotel Nacional, features comfortable, spacious bedrooms that are unfortunately subject to street noise. The hosts, both former engineers, make it their business to address their guests' every need.

Casa Alicia
$ **2 rooms**
(Map IV, A1).*104 Calle F, between Avenidas 5 and 7 (Calzada), close to the Malecón. (7) 832 0671. AC.*
You'll find a warm welcome at this nicely maintained apartment.

Rooms are small, but very clean, with plenty of storage space. Breakfast and dinner (if you wish) are served on the covered patio. If Alicia is full, the upstairs belongs to a retired couple, Gisela Ibarra and Daniel Rivero *(7 832 3238)*; one of their rooms has a private terrace.

Iliana García
$ **2 rooms**
(Map IV, A2). *554 Calle 2, between Calles 23 and 25. (7) 831 3329.*
Rooms here occupy a pleasant, clean and airy house graced with a front porch. Guests share a bathroom with the family; be prepared to wait a bit in the mornings. The hosts serve an abundant breakfast.

Silvia Vidal
$ **2 rooms**
(Map IV, A2). *602 Paseo, between Calles 25 and 27. (7) 833 4165. silviavidal602@yahoo.es. AC. Private Bathroom. TV. Breakfast between 3-5 CUC.*
This superb house, vintage 1925, offers spacious, nicely kept rooms, including one with a separate guest entrance.

Zoyla Zayas Ulloa
$ **2 rooms**
(Map IV, A1). *Apt. 1, 254 Calle K, between Calles 15 and 17. (7) 831 1764. AC.*
This lovely home, dating from 1925, has a terrace overlooking a balustraded garden on a tree-lined street. Mosquitoes can be a problem thanks to the resident cat, who chases the (mosquito-eating) geckos. Within the bedrooms, fans keep insects at bay. The resident parrot screeches when hungry but the hostess

never allows the noise to continue. The smaller of the two rooms is adequate for one person.

Hotels

Hotel Presidente
$$$ **158 rooms**
(Map IV, A1). *110 Ave. Calzada at corner of Ave. de los Presidentes. (7) 838 1801. www.hotelesc.com. TV. Breakfast included. 2 Restaurants. Swimming Pool.*
A grand full-service hotel, the Presidente offers clean rooms in a smart ambience. The attentive staff will see to all your needs.

Hotel Victoria
$$$ **31 rooms**
(Map IV, B1) .*101 Calle 19 with Calle M. (7) 833 3510. www.gran-caribe. com. TV. Breakfast included. Restaurant. Swimming Pool.*
This small hotel, with its attentive staff, has a cozy ambience. Ask for one of the corner rooms for double the street views.

🏛 Hotel Nacional
$$$$ **457 rooms**
(Map IV, B1). *Corner of Calles 12 and 0. (7) 836 3564. www.hotel nacionaldecuba.com. TV. Breakfast included. 3 Restaurants. 2 swimming pools.*
Located on the fringe of the Malecón, the Nacional is the most famous hotel in the city. Today a full-service hotel, it was built in 1930 and fully renovated during the 1990s. The sumptuous entrance hall and side salons lead to a pleasant garden, overlooking the Malecón, that is a favorite spot for mojitos and music. Guest rooms are somewhat plain; ask for one with a view of the sea.

Room with view, TRYP Habana Libre
©Sol Meliá Cuba

TRYP Habana Libre
$$$$ **572 rooms**
(Map IV, B1-2). *Calle L, between Calles 23-25. (7) 834 6158. www.solmeliacuba.com. TV. Breakfast included. Full board available. 4 Restaurants. Swimming Pool.*
This 25-story tower, formerly a Hilton hotel, has become the dominant feature of La Rampa. Recently renovated guest rooms offer every comfort, and a full slate of tourist services is available. If your budget allows, opt for one of the rooms with a panoramic view.

MIRAMAR
You'll need a vehicle or taxi to get to this neighborhood, which is located some distance southwest of downtown Havana.

Private Homes

🏛 Candy Mederos y Alejandro
$ **2 rooms**
(Map V, B1-2). *4408 Ave. 39, between Calles 44 and 46. (7) 203 6958. alejandroalvm@yahoo.com.*
Imposing on the outside and spacious on the inside, this home features a floor of polished granite in a geometric black and white pattern. The staircase leading to

the guest rooms has a majestic air. Breakfast (4CUC) is served in the salon or in the garden, in the shade of mango and avocado trees. A garage is available if you need it.

Hotels

Hotel Chateau Miramar
$$$$ **50 rooms**
(Map V, A1). *Avenida 1, between Calles 60 and 70. (7) 204 1952. www.hotelescubanacan.com. TV. Breakfast included. Restaurant. Swimming Pool.*
This small, modern seaside hotel bears no resemblance to a colonial fort, despite its grandiose name. Rather, it's a haven for business tourists, complete with meeting and conference rooms and office services. Guests here enjoy warm, attentive service. In-room Wi-Fi is a plus (and a rarity) in Cuba.

PLAYAS DEL ESTE
Most hotels for international visitors are in Santa María del Mar, the nicest of the beaches. Rates include breakfast. Guanabo's hotels welcome Cubans and international guests. Most hotels are close to the beach, and many have **swimming pools**.

Hotels

Blau Club Arenal
$$$ **169 rooms**
Laguna Itabo. (7) 797 1272. www.blau-hotels.com.
This modern resort complex is tucked into the natural curve of a pretty lagoon; a wooden bridge leads to the beach. You'll find good service here, a nice welcome and pleasant rooms, with an all-inclusive plan that includes

multiple activities. The resort is popular with Europeans and Canadians. Car rental. Internet.

Tropicoco
$$$ **188 rooms**
Avenida de las Terrazas and Avenida Banderas, Santa María del Mar. (7) 797 1371.
This huge Le Corbusier-esque beachside hotel features a pleasant lobby festooned with plants, although the guest rooms are rather plain. Try to get an ocean-view room with a balcony. Tourist services and Internet are available to guests as well as travelers not staying here. One of the liveliest of the hotels in the area.

Atlántico
$$$$ **92 rooms**
Intersection of Ave. de las Terrazas and Calle 11, Santa María del Mar. (7) 797 1085. www.gran-caribe.com.
Not to be confused with the Aparthotel of the same name over the road, this hotel is Santa María del Mar's only property located directly on a lovely swathe of beach. It's one of the nicer hotels along the east beaches, with clean, pleasant rooms (those on the ground floor are too low for views of the sea). Rates include all meals and sporting activities; there is also a swimming pool. The property is often booked by Italian tourists, except in off-season.

Super-Club Breezes
$$$$ **250 rooms**
Playa Arrojo Bermejo, KM 60 Via Blanca, Santa Cruz del Norte. (4) 729 5122. www.superclub scuba.com.
This deluxe all-inclusive resort at **Playa Jibacoa** is nicely situated

between the hills and, effectively, a private beach. A wide variety of sports activities is available, including snorkeling and diving, and there's a large swimming pool. Book through a travel agent to get the best rates. The property is very popular with British and Canadian travelers, and is conveniently located close to Havana. Every service is available.

⛱ Villa Los Pinos
$$$$ 24 bungalows
Avenida de los Terrazas, between Calles 4 and 5, Santa María del Mar (7) 797 1361. www.gran-caribe.com.
A rare find in Cuba, these old villas, scattered more off the beach than on, have 2 to 4 bedrooms joined by a living room. Some feature small swimming pools. Prices vary depending on the amenities and proximity to the beach. Facilities need updating, however.

VARADERO
It is now possible to rent legal *casas particulares* in Varadero. Many of the hotels are all-inclusive (meals included in the rate); be sure to ask in advance.

Hotels

Acuazul
$ 78 rooms
(Map I, B1-2). *Corner of Ave. 1ra and Calles 13 and 14. (4) 566 7132. www.islazul.com. TV. 2 restaurants. Swimming pool.*
This large, rather austere building dates from before the Revolution. Guest rooms are clean and spacious, with balconies, and there's a small swimming pool. Reasonable rates, even if a bit higher than the adjacent complex

formed by the Varazul and Villa Sotavento hotels. Car rental, currency exchange, medical service.

Dos Mares
$ 34 rooms
(Map I, E1). *Corner of Ave. 1ra and Calle 53. (4) 566 7161. www.islazul.cu. TV. Breakfast included. Restaurant.*
This pretty tile-roofed hotel in downtown Varadero offers clean, if dated, rooms. It's a good choice for single travelers. Reserve well in advance. Currency exchange, car rental.

Herradura
$ 75 rooms
(Map I, D1). *Avenida de la Playa, between Calles 35 and 36. (4) 561 3703. TV. Breakfast included. Restaurant.*
This horseshoe-shaped building (*herradura* in Spanish) boasts a pleasant terrace overlooking the sea. Budget apartments include 2 to 5 bedrooms and a common room; guests share apartments in high season. Guest rooms are quite dated and worn, but this is a budget bargain, since it's the only hotel in this price range actually on the beach. Currency exchange.

⛱ Pullman
$ 16 rooms
(Map I, E1). *Corner of Ave. 1ra and Calle 49. (4) 566 7161. www.islazul.cu. TV. Breakfast included. Restaurant.*
This small, family-style hotel just 150m/164ft from the beach offers rooms in a charming old stone building, or in a modern annex at the rear. The hotel shares

the same facilities with the Dos Mares hotel located down the street.

Club Kawama

$$$$ **336 rooms**

(Map I, A1). *Primera Avenida and Calle 1, Reparto Kawama. (4) 561 4416. www.gran-caribe.com. TV. 3 restaurants. Swimming pool.*
Located at the entrance to Varadero, between the Paso Malo lagoon and a peaceful beach, the hotel comprises stone buildings dating before the Revolution, along with more recent additions. If possible, ask for number 420, overlooking the sea. This well regarded hotel is a popular spot with German tourists.

Los Delfines

$$$$ **103 rooms**

(Map I, D1). *Corner of Avenida de la Playa and Calle 39. (4) 566 7720. www.islazul.cu. TV. Restaurant. Swimming pool.*
This hotel in the center of Varadero is easy to spot thanks to its green and candy-pink façade. Guest rooms in the antique stone building and its more modern seaside annex are spacious and comfortable. Welcoming staff.

Hotel Mercure Cuatro Palmas

$$$$ **282 rooms**

(Map I, F1). *Avenida 1, between Calles 60 and 62. (4) 566 7040. www.accorhotels.com. TV. 2 restaurants. Swimming pool.*
This immense, colonial-style building sports verdant plants and tropical birds in the lovely entry hall. The atmosphere is quiet and pleasant; the all-inclusive plan is a good value. The Cuatro Palmas runs an additional small hotel across the street, where the guest rooms are clean and simple.

Villa Tortuga

$$$$ **292 rooms**

(Map I, A2). *Calle 7 and Avenida Kawama. (4) 561 4747. www.gran-caribe.com. TV. 2 restaurants. Swimming pool.*
This fine resort complex extends along the coast between Calles 5 and 8. Spacious rooms occupy individual villas situated between the beach and the swimming pool. Games and activities are organized on the beach, along with Cuban-flavored shows and salsa-dancing lessons. Moped rental.

HICACOS PENINSULA

Since the early 1990s, the foreign hotel chains have erected large, luxurious resorts at the eastern end of the Varadero peninsula. These hotels maintain similar standards of service, facilities and amenities, and offer all-inclusive packages (reserve through a travel agent to get the best rates). They are located some distance from Varadero town center.

Hotels

Varadero Internacional

$$$ **162 rooms**

Avenida de las Américas (after Calle 69). (4) 566 7038. www.gran-caribe.com. TV. Restaurant. Swimming pool.
Varadero's premier hotel, built in the 1950s, maintains its retro charm. A broad terrace extends toward a beautiful beach. Rooms

are comfortable. If you can, reserve magnificent rooftop suites 601 or 602; both can be booked for the same price as a regular room.

Arenas Blancas
$$$$ 358 rooms
Calle 64 between 1ra and Autopista. (4) 561 4450. www.barcelo.com. TV. 9 restaurants. Swimming Pool.
Located on the beach at the easternmost point within the city limits, the Arenas Blancas belongs to the Barceló hotel chain. Excellent service. Rooms are very pleasant in an otherwise unremarkable building.

Mansión Du Pont de Nemours (Xanadú)
$$$$$ 8 rooms
8.5km along the Carretera between Las Morlas and Varadero. (4) 566 8482. www.varaderogolfclub.com. TV. Breakfast included. Restaurant.
Overlooking the waterfront on one side and the Varadero Golf Club on the other, this hotel offers interesting accommodations. Spacious rooms have sea views, 1930s-era furnishings and marble bathrooms. The rooftop bar offers a great view, and live music nightly *(except Sunday)*.

Meliá Las Américas
**$$$$$ 250 rooms and
                82 bungalows**
Carretera de las Morlas. (4) 566 7600. www.solmeliacuba.com. TV. 5 restaurants. Swimming pool.
Golfers at the adjacent links frequent this popular, full-service hotel that sits amid well-manicured gardens on a prime stretch of stunning beachfront.

Lobby, Meliá Varadero

©Sol Meliá Cuba

🛏 Meliá Varadero
$$$$$ 490 rooms
Km 7.5 Autopista Sur. (4) 566 7013. www.solmeliacuba.com. TV. 5 restaurants. Swimming pool.
An enormous pyramidal structure houses one of the peninsula's most luxurious resorts.

Paradisus Varadero
$$$$$ 510 rooms
Punta Rincón Francés, between Autopista Sur and Cueva de Ambrosio. (4) 566 8700. TV. Spa. 7 restaurants. 2 swimming pools.
Pleasant bungalows house bright guest rooms at one of the most luxurious (and expensive) properties in Varadero, located at the northern tip of the peninsula, just steps from the wilderness. Watersports, tennis, golf and many other recreational activities. Spa services and a fitness center.

HOTELS

HAVANA

A

Accessibility 31
Acuario National de Cuba 66
Afro-Cuban music 90
Airlines 27
Airport 27
Alacio de los Condes de
  Casa Bayona 45
Almacenes San José 14
Alonso, Alicia 85, 112
Arena Rafael Trejo 111
Art Galleries 122
Asociación Cultura Yoruba de
  Cuba 90, 94, 115
Avenida Primera (Avenida 1) 65

B

Ballet Nacional
  de Cuba 112
Banks 33
Barrio Chino 58
Bars 124
Baseball 111
Basic Information 32
Basilica Menor y Convento de
  San Francisco de Asís 49
Batista, Fulgencio 79
Beaches 96
Bicycles 31
Blanck, Hubert De 64
Boating 108
Bobadilla, Doña Isabel de 74
Bosque de la Habana 67
Boxing 111
Buena Vista Social Club 89
Bus 29

C

Cabaret 91
Cabaret Parisien 91
Calendar of events 18
Callejón de Hamel 59, 89

Calle Obispo 47
Calle Oficios 48
Capitolio Nacional 55, 69
Car rental 31
Carpentier, Alejo 64
Casa de Guayasamín 86
Casa de Pérez de la Riva 85
Casa de la Amistad 89
Casa de la Condesa de la
  Reunió 44
Casa de la Música Habana 88
Casa de las Hermanas Cárdenas 50
Casa de los Arabes 48
Casa de los Marqueses de Aguas
  Claras 42
Casa del Conde de Jaruco 51
Casa del Conde de Lombillo 44
Casas particulares 128, 140
Castro, Fidel 13, 18, 20, 38, 39, 48,
  58, 63, 78, 86
Castro, Raul 86
Castillo de la Real Fuerza 74
Castillo de los Tres Reyes
  del Morro 76
Castillo de San Salvador de la
  Punta 75
Castillo del Príncipe 63
Catedral de San Cristóbal 41, 68
Cementerio de Cristóbal Colón 63
Centro de Arte Contemporáneo
  Wifredo Lam 86
Centro Habana 54
Céspedes, Carlos Manuel de 45, 78
Chacón, Luis 45
Chinatown 58
Cienfuegos, Camilo 80
Cigars 117, 118
Ciudad Deportiva 111
Club de Golf Habana 109
Conjunto Folklórico Nacional
  de Cuba 16, 114
Convento de Santa Clara 51

INDEX

Convento de Nuestra Señora
de la Merced 52
Convento de Nuestra Señora
de Belén 53
Coppelia 61, 72
Cuban Classics 68
Cuban Revolution 38
Cubanacán 69, 141
Cueva Ambrosio 105
Cuevas de Bellamar
(Bellamar Caves) 106
Cuisine 130
Currency Exchange 33
Customs Regulations 26

D

Danza Contemporánea
de Cuba 115
Delfinario 104
Delirio Habanero 90
Depósito del automóvil 48
Districts 40
Diving 108
Dominoes 111
Drinks 131
Duncan, John H. 65

E

Eastern Beaches 98
Edificio Bacardí 72
Edificio Focsa 61
EGREM 88
Templete, El 47
Emergencies 30
Entry Requirements 24
Escalona, Salvador González 59
Estadio Latinoamericano 111
Excursions 100

F

Fábrica de Tabacos Partagás 58
Factoria Habana 86

Farmacia y Droguería Taquechel 47
Fishing 109
Flamenco 125
Forestier, Jean-Claude Nicolas 93
Fortaleza de San Carlos de
la Cabaña 76
Fuentes, Gregorio 87
Fundación Cultural Alejo
Carpentier 44
Fundación Havana Club 50

G

Getting Around 28
Getting There 27
Golf 109
Gómez, Máximo 79
Gran Teatro de La Habana 70
Guanabo 98
Guevara, Che 38, 77, 80, 119, 121

H

Habana Vieja, La 40
Habaguanex 37
Hatuey 78
Havana Club 131
Health 26
Hemingway, Ernest 15, 19, 67, 87
Hicacos Peninsula 100, 104
Hiking 110
Hotel Moka 107
Hotel Nacional 61, 72, 89
Hotels
   Centro Habana
     Deauville 145
     Casa 1932 145
   La Habana Vieja
     Ambos Mundos 143
     Beltrán de Santa Cruz 143
     Casa Colonial Azul 141
     Casa Dos Hermanas Yonaika
     y Yonaisis 141
     Casa Humberto 141

INDEX

Casa Maritza Mirabal y
Ramón 141
Conde de Villanueva 143
Convento de Santa Brígida y
Madre Isabel 142
Eugenio y Fabio 141
Hostal Valencia 143
Hotel Florida 143
Hotel Inglaterra 143
Hotel Parque Central 144
Hotel Plaza 143
Hotel Santa Isabel 47, 145
Hotel Saratoga 145
Hotel Tejadillo 144
Jesús y María 142
Mercure Sevilla 71, 144
Nancy Pérez 142
Olga López Hernández 142
Palacio del Marqués de San
Felipe y Santiago de
Bejucal 145
Palacio O'Farrill 144
Residencia Académica
Convento de Santa
Clara 142
Hicacos Peninsula
Arenas Blancas 151
Mansión Du Pont de Nemours
(Xanadú) 151
Meliá Las Américas 151
Meliá Varadero 151
Paradisus Varadero 151
Varadero Internacional 151
Miramar
Candy Mederos y
Alejandro 148
Hotel Chateau Miramar 148
Playas del Este
Atlántico 148
Blau Club Arenal 148
Super-Club Breezes 149
Tropicoco 148
Villa Los Pinos 149
Las Terrazas
Hotel Moka 107

Varadero
Acuazul 149
Club Kawama 150
Dos Mares 149
Herradura 149
Hotel Mercure Cuatro
Palmas 150
Los Delfines 150
Pullman 150
Villa Tortuga 150
Vedado
Alejandro Martínez 146
Amparo López 146
Armando y Betty
Gutiérrez 146
Casa Alicia 146
Hotel Nacional 147
Hotel Presidente 147
Hotel Victoria 147
Iliana García 146
Silvia Vidal 146
TRYP Habana Libre 61, 147
Zoyla Zayas Ulloa 146

I

Iglesia de San Francisco
de Paula 53
Iglesia del Espíritu Santo 52
Iglesia y Convento de Nuestra
Señora de Belén 53
Iglesia y Convento de Nuestra
Señora de la Merced 53
Information, Basic 32
Instituto Superior del
Arte School 69
Internet 32

J

Jardín Botánico Nacional
de Cuba 95
Jelengue de Areito, El 91, 126
Jineteros 125

K

Know before you go 23
Kohly District 67

INDEX

L

La Habana Vieja 40
Lam, Wifredo 83, 86
Landmarks with a beat 88
Las Terrazas 107
Lenin, Vladimir 94
Lessons and Classes 15, 16
Lonja del Comercio 49

M

Mail 33
Malecón 54
Mansión Du Pont de Nemours
 (Mansión Xanadú) 104
Maqueta de La Ciudad 65
Marina Hemingway 67, 108
Martí, José 81
Matanzas 99, 105
Memorial de José Martí 80
Miramar 65
Money 33
Monument to the Victims
 of USS Maine 61
Moré, Benny 48, 91
Museo Antropológico
 Montané 62
Museo de Arte Colonial 45
Museo de la Ciudad 45, 46
Museo de Artes Decorativas 84
Museo de la Cerámica
 Contemporánea Cubana 84
Museo de la Comandancia del
 Che Guevara 77
Museo de la Danza 85
Museo de la Revolución 79
Museo del Chocolate 50
Museo Farmaceútico 106
Museo Hemingway 87
Museo José Martí - Casa Natal
 de José Martí 86
Museo del Ministerio del
 Interior 65
Museo Municipal 103
Museo Nacional de Bellas Artes
 (Arte Cubano) 83

Museo Nacional de Bellas Artes
 (Arte Universal) 82
Museo Nacional de Historia
 Natural 48
Museo Nacional de la Música 85
Museo Napoleónico 63, 86
Museums 82

N

Nemours, Francis Irénée
 Du Pont de 104
Nightlife 124
Nuevo Vedado 60

O

Orishas 90, 94
Outdoor Life 108

P

Palacio Abiscopal 48
Palacio de la Revolución 81
Palacio de los Capitanes
 Generales 45
Palacio del Conde de
 Santovenia 47
Palacio del Marqués de Arcos 44
Palacio del Segundo Cabo 46
Palacio Presidencial 79
Paladares 129
Parks and Gardens 92
Parque Central 92
Parque Céspedes 78
Parque Emiliano Zapata 65
Parque de la Fraternidad 93
Parque de los Mártires 78
Parque Histórico Militar
 Morro Cabaña 77
Parque Lenin 94
Performing Arts 112
Piso 9 115
Planetario 50
Playa Jibacoa 99
Playa Santa María del Mar 96, 98
Playas del Este 96
Playita del 16 65
Plaza de Armas 45

Plaza de la Catedral 41
Plaza de la Revolución 63, 80
Plaza de San Francisco de Asís 48
Plaza Vieja 50
Police 30
Portocarrero, René, 14, 64, 84, 94
Practical Information 22
Prado, The 55
Punta Hicacos Sector 105
Puppet shows 115

Q
Quinta Avenida (Avenida 5) 65

R
Rampa, La 60
Religion 39
Restaurants 128
  Ruinas, La 94
    Centro Habana
    Asahi 134
    Castropol 134
    La Guarida 134
    San Cristobal 134
    La Habana Vieja
    Al Medina 132
    Café Escorial 133
    Café Lamparilla 133
    Café O'Reilly 133
    Café del Oriente 133
    Café Taberna 91
    El Floridita 133
    El Mesón de la Flota 132
    El Patio 133
    El Templete 133
    La Barca 132
    La Bodeguita del Medio 131
    La Casa de la Parra 131
    La Imprenta 132
    La Moneda 132
    La Mulata del Sabor 132
    La Taberna de la Muralla 132
    Roof Garden Torre
      del Oro 134
    Torre la Vega 131

Miramar and Playa
Doctor Café 137
El Aljibe 137
El Palenque 136
El Palio 137
El Tocororo 138
La Cecilia 137
La Cocina de Lilliam 137
La Ferminia 137
La Paila 138
Nuevo Vedado
Restaurante La Casa 136
Playas del Este
Mi Cayito 138
Piccolo Paladar 138
Pizzeria Don Peppo 138
Varadero
El Bodegón Criollo 139
Casa del Chef, La 139
Castel Nuovo 138
El Mesón del Quijote 139
El Restaurante Xanadú 139
Ranchón El Compay 139
Retiro Josone 139
Vega, La 139
Vedado
Atelier 135
Café Cantante 88
Café Laurent 135
Casona de 17, La 135
El Gringo Viejo 136
La Rampa 135
Los Amigos 135
Monguito 135
Nerei 135
Restaurante 1830 136
Unión Francesa de Cuba 136
Retiro Josone 103
Revolutionary Sites 78
Roman Catholicism 39
Rum 120

INDEX

S

Sábado de la
  Rumba 90
Sánchez, Celia 94
Santería 39, 59, 90
Segundo, Compay 89
Shopping 116
Sierra del Rosario 107
Smoking 34
Sores, Jacques de 77
Souvenirs 121
Spanish Forts 74

T

Taxes 34
Taxis 30
Teatro Amadeo
  Roldán 113
Teatro América 73
Teatro Karl Marx 114
Teatro Lírico
  Nacional 112
Teatro Mella 115
Teatro Nacional 113
Teatro Sauto 106
Telephones 34
Temperatures 22

Ten Years War 78
Tennis 110
Tipping 34, 128
Toilets, Public 35
Tourism offices 23
Tourist Assistance 24
Tourist Card 25
Tours 12, 13,14, 15
Trains 29
Tropicana 91

U

UNESCO World
  Heritage Site 39, 40
Universidad de La
  Habana 62

V

Vaccinations 25
Varadero 100
Vedado 60
Vermay, Jean-Baptiste
  47, 68
Viñes, Benito 53
Villaverde, Cirilo 64
Visa extension 25

W

Water, Drinking 35
Water Sports 110
Weather forecasts 22
When to go 22
Wi Fi 33

Y

Yumuri Valley 99

Z

Zaldívar, Antonio
  Fernández de
  Trebejos y 46
Zorra y el Cuervo, La
  91, 127

List of Maps

La Habana Area *inside front cover*
La Habana Vieja, Historic Center *40*
La Habana Vieja *43*
La Habana, Vedado-Centro
  Habana *56-57*
Cementerio de Cristóbal Colón *64*

La Habana, Miramar and Playa *66*
The North Coast *98-99*
Varadero *102 103*
Península de Hicacos *104-105*
Island of Cuba *inside back cover*

Photo Credits (page Icons)

INDEX